MW00718129

The Breakup Guide

How to Get Over It in half the time

By Baje Fletcher

Edited By Michael S. Nixon & Angel De Souza

GLITZ & GLAMOUR PUBLISHING

Glitz & Glamour

MikeNixon.politocomm@gmail.com

ISBN# 978-0-9911608-0-8

Dedicated to:

All those trying to find their heart's
RESET button!

Table of Contents

Acknowledgements 5

Introduction 11

Chapter One: Screw Father Time 15

Chapter Two: Let it Burn 35

Chapter Three: I Love Me Too Much! 61

Chapter Four: 30 days to Happiness 109

Chapter five: Get It Together 131

Chapter Six: When the Shoe is on The Other Foot 145

Chapter Seven: Finding Courage & Closure 157

Chapter Eight: Be Wiser 169

Chapter Nine: How to Pick a Better Mate 177

Chapter Ten: Your New Life Begins Now 183

<u>Acknowledgements</u>

I still can't believe that my first book is on shelves! It's amazing that a seed so small, planted in my mind, could grow into an actual product so big that it found itself into the homes of thousands of women all over the world. Mr. James Cannon (father to Nick Cannon), I thanked you in my first book and I'm thanking you again because that's just how much you mean to me.

I remember when I first moved to Los Angeles, you asked me what brought me to LA. I told you acting and modeling. You gave me a look like you weren't surprised. You said, "Sweetie, you're beautiful and I'm sure you're talented, but millions of beautiful, talented women come to LA to pursue the same thing. Have you thought about writing?" For a split second apart of me wanted to retaliate and say something along the lines of "I'll make it, you'll see". But before I could, my brain kicked out a memory of a conversation I had with two of my girlfriends about six months prior. I was always the 'go to' girl among my friends when it came to matters of men money and makeovers. So as we sat in my living room on what seemed like a Saturday afternoon, the girls picked my brain about how I was able to get the things I wanted from men and still be able to dodge the sex-trap. After talking to them for an hour or so, one of them blurted out, "Girl, you should write a book!". We brain stormed for book titles. I shouted out, "Get His Cash & Make A Dash?" We laughed that title off. Then I decided on: A Goal Digger's Guide - How to Get What You Want, without Giving IT Up. That was it! Immediately I grabbed my laptop and began typing away. After a page of typing we started discussing other things and I got distracted. Just like that, the seed was forgotten...until I met you **Mr. Cannon**. I remember hesitating as I told you the title of that book that laid dormant in my mind. I thought that the idea would have fallen on deaf ears, but it did not. Your eyes lit up as you replied "Sweetie, finish it. It's going to be a best seller!" For the next two weeks you watered that seed by checking up on my progress. Every other day you called and asked, "Sweetie is it done yet? I'm excited to read it". Because of your faith in me the book was completed. **Thanks Mr. Cannon.**

Since the first copy was released women have been writing to me from all over the world. It's truly a humbling experience. With my first book, my biggest struggle was deciding if I should share my personal experiences and parts of my delicate childhood with the world. Even though I knew some of the information I shared could be used in debates against me, I decided that it was the right thing to do. My readers deserved to know about my fears and my struggles in order to truly understand where I came from and how I adapted my mentality. After all, no one wants to take advice from someone who they can't relate to. My decision to share my shortcomings proved to be the right decision because women of all ages, from all over the globe have shared intimate details of their own struggles with me. By making my life literally an open book, I have connected with women who I never would have connected with otherwise. Through sharing my life story I've acquired **fans & friends (some of who feel like family)...and to you all I'm beyond grateful.** Thanks for the letters, the e-mails, the blogs, the videos, the Twitter retweets, the Facebook shares, the Instagram likes, and especially the reviews on Amazon, Audible, BarnesAndNoble.com, and on all the other sites where my book is available. You all mean so much to me!

I almost forgot to **thank my critics.** If you hate to see me do well, then you're really going to hate me now. I don't know what it is about someone doubting my ability that makes me want to prove them wrong. I remember doing my first radio interview; It was in Orlando on the "Monsters in the Morning" radio station. When I told the host that I wrote a book, he asked me who the publisher was and after telling him that I was self-publishing he made a spectacle of me and told his listeners that my book would never make it past the copy machine at Kinkos!! Only a few months later imagine how shocked he was when he heard that my book was available in Barnes & Noble bookstores all over the US!!

All I had was a dream, but luckily, that dream was all I needed.

THE BREAKUP GUIDE

Introduction

Every time someone left my life and I felt like a big piece of me was gone (whether it was because of relocation, a breakup, or death of a loved one), I told myself,

"Keep it moving", you'll be okay."

Many times I didn't believe it at that very moment but I knew that no matter what, I had to keep moving. I had to drag one heavy foot in front of the other in hopes that I'd be able to run again someday. At times I had no idea what direction to go in, but I knew I couldn't stay in the same spot. I felt like if I stopped striving then I'd be stuck in that sad place forever. The main thought that kept me from falling into depression was thinking of my mother. One vivid image held me captive: Her sitting in the middle of the living room of a half furnished home…with only half of her heart remaining. It was the day her and my dad separated; until the day she died she never fully recovered from the separation. I refused to become that broken hearted woman.

Dear Baje years ago I was deeply in love; in hindsight I loved him for all the wrong reasons. He never deserved me but because I was blinded by lust he seemed to be my everything. If I didn't hear from him one day, I couldn't eat, sleep or think straight; he had that much of a hold on me. If my phone rang and it wasn't him, then I wasn't picking it up. My patience was short and my temper was even shorter and if I didn't hear from him I was snapping on everyone. I remember at one point in time I didn't hear from him for three days and I could hardly find the energy to leave my bedroom. When I finally heard from him I was so happy, I felt like I could move mountains. I didn't even bother to ask him where he was for the past few days; I was just happy that he resurfaced. Over the next few months he repeated that pattern a few more times. Then one day he called me out of the blue and told me that that he couldn't see me anymore – just like that! (I played that scenario in my head hundreds of times throughout our 'relationship' because it was my worst fear). Whenever I would express that fear to him he assured me that he'd never leave me. When I got that phone call tears streamed down my face; I was in shock! I kept repeating to myself, "This can't be happening, he cant be serious". Well...he was serious and he didn't want me anymore POINT BLANK PERIOD. After all the years, all that I invested in us and after all of the promises he made, he couldn't just leave me like that! Well he could, and guess what? He did: March 9th 2008. For a minute I thought I was going to die, for a split second I didn't care if I did...and then I looked at my 3 year old. She was asleep; she was laying on the bed beside me. I was crushed but I had to be strong for her. Yes I loved him, but I loved her so more. I cuddled up beside her and thanked God for what I DID have, and that was my daughter and her unconditional love.

Looking back, I can't believe that I gave a man that much power over my thoughts, emotions, actions and life. It took self-discipline and months of hard work for me to be emotionally independent, but I finally achieved it. I'll never ever depend on someone else for my happiness again.

- Alethia

Chapter 1

Screw Father Time

Screw Father Time

Getting over anyone is effortless; all you have to do is just not think about them. THE END. Okay, okay, all jokes aside, getting over someone isn't easy but it's definitely possible.

First thing's first: Do you remember your friends, the friends you use to hang with and call everyday before you found a man? You know those friends you ditched once you fell in love? Yeah. Now its time to go crawling back and start begging for their friendship because you're going to need them for some emotional support. Granted, they may feel a bit rejected; but if they're true friends they'll take you back...after they make you jump through a few hoops.

They say that time heals all wounds but it's not the time that heals, it's *what you do with that time* that makes all the difference. The prescription for your broken heart is to *believe* that you deserve better.

Not to just say it, but to truly mean it. Once you do, then you'll clearly see that wasting time and energy worrying about someone who doesn't deserve you is senseless. When you've come to that realization, then it's time to replace him with other memories. I'll teach you some self-esteem building exercises as well that will help you to find yourself again.

Eventually most of us will get over a breakup but who wants to wait for "eventually"? With a little help from me, my research and the interviews I've conducted you're going to get over him in half the time it would take you to do so by yourself.

SO THE LOVE BUG HAS BITTEN YOU

It's not a matter of *if* we'll fall for someone or not; we're human and one day we'll all take that tumble (whether it's off a chair or off a cliff). Life isn't scored by our falls, but by how fast we bounce back, hop back on our feet and jump back into the game. Whether is a short crush or a long-term relationship, If we live long enough we're bound to go through it. Once Cupid leaves and the pretty little butterflies turn into big black moths we all go looking for a quick fix to erase him from our memories. How do we escape the sick feeling when his name is mentioned or how emotional we get when we see someone that looks like him? We do so by recognizing that we have the power to control our thoughts.

Lesson: #1. You are not your mind.

Here's proof: can you recall a time when a thought popped in your mind, and you told yourself that you shouldn't do or say that, so you talked yourself out of it? That proves that you and your mind are two entirely different entities. Based on what we hear, see, experience or are taught throughout our lives our mind *suggests* things; but we don't always have to do what it suggests. We can *train* our minds.

Think of your mind as a whining nagging child crying for some candy. You may feel pressured to give into the tantrum, but you *know* it's not the best thing to do so decide not to. Our minds may say: I don't have the energy, I feel sad or I don't feel like getting out of bed. Most of the time we just give in to our thoughts because it's easier at that very moment; however, that brief choice of giving in can hurt us in the long run. The good news is the breakthrough moment you realize you are *not* your mind, then your life gets so much better. You'll be able to make conscious decisions to do what you know you NEED to do and not just cave in to your thoughts. If you feel like staying in bed, instead, get your MP3 player, put on some upbeat music and tell yourself that you are going to go jogging. At first it may be hard, but the more you do it, the easier it gets. Soon your mind will begin to see who's the boss and will have no choice but to tag along.

Before we go any further, let me assure you that I know what you are going through. I wasn't always this "no nonsense diva" with a backbone of titanium. Let's just say that I too have had my share of disappointments. Even though the hardest part of this process is going to be *not* thinking about him, it would be unrealistic to set a goal to stop thinking about him instantly. Sorry, but there is no magic potion to mend a broken heart. The goal right now is to simply *cope.* Take it step-by-step; one day at a time. You have to force yourself to do things that take your mind off of him in increments. At first it may be one minute at a time, then 30 minutes, then a whole day. Before you know it you'll go *days* then *weeks* without thinking about him.

<u>Lesson: #2.</u> *You can control your feelings, both good and bad.*

You have to learn to control your thoughts because your thoughts control your emotions and your emotions dictate your actions. If you just lay in bed, you'll continue to feel sad, and by being stuck in those same thoughts, you'll be trapped in those same emotions.

Breakups really suck! It seems like he's the first thing on your mind when you wake up and the last thing on your mind when you go to sleep. Sadly, staying asleep as long as possible doesn't work either because when you sleep, you dream of him. Don't you wish life had a reset button?

Look at yourself! Your hair is a mess, you haven't showered in days and you have no motivation to do *anything*. Get a hold of yourself. I know you didn't deserve being dumped, or perhaps you were the one who called it quits because things just weren't working; either way...It's time to get over it!

You have to *want* to get over it; I mean *really want* to get over it. If you're still seeking revenge or on Twitter trying to figure out how to 'accidentally' run into him, then honey, you don't *really* want to get over him.

Lesson: #3. Your thoughts control your feelings and your feelings control your actions.

Think about it: Have you ever eaten something that you previously said you'd never eat, but one day you ate it without knowing what it was and you were perfectly fine while you were eating it; and it wasn't until *after* you found out what you were actually eating that you felt disgusted? Or how about that one thing you had that you never used? It just sat in your closet collecting dust? Once you finally gave it away and were told how valuable it was, all of a sudden you secretly wished you kept it. Well it's kind of the same thing. Often times it's not the actual event that bothers us but it's what we *think* of it that does. Its all a matter of perspective.

A study that was done with toddlers showed that when they were placed in a room with a snake they behaved normally. They even crawled over to the snake out of curiosity and weren't even afraid to touch it. Minutes later their parents were brought into the room and fear was on every parents' faces It wasn't until the toddlers looked at their parent's reactions that they began to fear the snake.

Lesson: #4. _Most things are mind over matter. If you don't mind it will not matter._

When your heart is breaking and you're longing for that person who was supposed to be your other half, the last thing that you want to hear is: "time heals all wounds".

Well, time may heal a physical wound but it doesn't mend a broken heart. _It's what you do with that time that counts._ If you spend that time looking at photos or videos of the person you're trying to get over, it will seem like time is standing still.

Lesson: #5. _You have the power to choose._

I learned that I had the power to control my feelings at age 19. My mother had just passed away from breast cancer, and even though it wasn't her fault I was still sad, hurt, frustrated and most of all angry. I quietly observed how my sister was able to handle all the funeral arrangements. She was sad also, but she was still able to push forward, think clearly and do what she had to do. On the other hand, I couldn't think straight, I couldn't speak without shouting. I was snapping at everyone as if it were their fault. The day before the funeral service and I remember being in the passenger seat of my sister's car, she was driving. I looked over to my left and asked if she wasn't sad. She glanced over at me and said:

"Well, every time I think about the bad things I get sad and every time I think about the good times that I was able to share with mom then I feel happy; so I just *choose* to think about the good times".

At that very moment I learned one of life's greatest lessons. The keyword in her answer was "choose". We have the power to choose; each and every one of us. We can't always dictate what happens to us, but we can choose our thoughts while we are going through *any* situation.

Lesson: #6. **Life is 10% what happens to us, and 90% how we react to those things.**

THE SYMPTOMS

Men & women may handle breakups differently. Just because they don't react the same doesn't mean that they're not experiencing the same emotions. Following a breakup, you may go through a whole range of negative emotions and some of those emotions may make you do things that you normally would not do. For instance, some people:

THE BREAKUP GUIDE

May take their frustrations out on others,

May not be able to sleep,

May sleep too much,

May not be able to eat,

May eat too much,

May think about hurting themselves,

May want to hurt others,

May spend your time plotting ways to get even,

May use drugs to cope,

My over indulge in alcohol,

May isolate themselves,

May have sex with people you normally wouldn't,

May turn away from sex completely,

May avoid the opposite   sex completely,

All these are unhealthy ways of coping. You'll to consciously work through these feelings to find positive ways to deal with the situation at hand.

THE MYTHS

Time heals all wounds – It's not *time* that heals, but it's what you do with your time that makes all the difference. The more time you spend thinking of that person, the longer it will take for you to get over them.

It takes half the amount of time that you were with that person to get over that person – Every situation varies and each person differs.

The breakup will affect your self-esteem - Someone else not wanting you has nothing to do with your self-worth, so their decision should NEVER affect how you feel about yourself.

You'll never find someone as good as him – that's a

load of crap! There are *millions* and *millions* of men in the world. You *can* and *will* find someone better suited for you when you are ready.

I need closure – Sure some closure or reasoning behind the breakup will help, but it's really not necessary.

Lesson: #7. **Don't get even, get over it.**

STARTING THE HEALING PROCESS

Some positive ways you can cope:

Try not to be alone.

Stay out of the house.

Move into a new place.

Get rid of all photos and paraphernalia that reminds you of your Ex (that includes the photos in your phone).

Block his phone number from calling or texting you.

Block him from your e-mail, and all social sites.

Change your phone number if he constantly tries to call you from different phone numbers.

Call an old friend to vent (but not one of your EXes).

Put on some upbeat music and make a video of you dancing. Oh you can't dance? That's even better. Just do something out of the ordinary that's fun and will have you laughing at yourself.

Make a workout video or participate in some activity that will give you an energy boost.

Stock your fridge with happy foods! Not necessarily unhealthy foods...it can be strawberries or whatever...but snacks that you love and things that make you feel good.

Find a new hobby or revisit an old one (dance, workout, yoga, baking, knitting, board games...something!)

Start a journal to keep a record of your feelings and progress throughout this breakup process.

Travel to a new place. It doesn't have to be out of the country, state or even the city. It can be 30 minutes away from your home. Just pack your bag and put yourself in a new environment for a day or two.

Start to write that book that you always wanted to write. It will keep your mind occupied. If you're not big on writing or typing then just start talking on your webcam and you can have someone type it up at a later date. You can even get a software program like *Dragon Naturally Speaking* that will type it as you speak. Writing and publishing a book these days is easier than it was ten years ago. The hardest part is getting started, so just get started.

Watch or listen to something productive (like self-help or audio cds). Learn a new language via an audio program or listen to a biography of someone who inspires you or someone who beat tremendous odds. If you are a Christian you can listen to the audio version of the Bible.

Always keep in mind those who depend on you for financial or emotional support. If you don't have anyone who depends on you then find things that create meaning in your life. Start a garden, get pets, (even fish) or just do something that puts you in an entirely different daily routine. Search for things that makes your life more meaningful.

Sign up with a charity and volunteer your time to those families who need help. You'll realize that your problems are super small compared to most people in this world.

Start cooking! Don't know how to cook? Great! Even better, you'll learn a new skill and will be busy experimenting and looking up so many recipes on the internet that it will take your mind off of things.

Discard of all the gifts, photos and memorabilia from your Ex. Sell them, give them away, it doesn't matter, just get rid of them.

If he bought you jewelry turn in the jewels for cash...(at a pawn shop, on Ebay or have a garage sale). Then put the money you make towards a personal goal of yours...like continuing your education or paying down debt.

If you are feeling unstable then take extra precautions by getting rid of any weapons or any extra prescription medications.

Cut off all contact and distance yourself from mutual friends...just until you get back to being your normal self.

Do not have sex with your Ex Period! This isn't like quitting smoking; There is no 'one last time'.

(because for most women, the more they have sex with a person the more attached they'll become).

If you need extra reinforcement then speak to a professional psychologist.

THE BREAKUP GUIDE

Chapter 2

Let it Burn

Let it Burn

The Breakup Process: There are different types of breakups...it can be a short crush, a parting with your high school sweetheart, the end of a long term relationship or an Ex-husband who you have children with (in that case it would be harder to cut the strings if you have ties that deep).

Denial – Generally speaking, people hate change. We hate to deal with the unknown, so naturally our minds want to cling to what we have grown accustomed to. You know the breakup is taking place but you refuse to accept it. This is one of the most detrimental phases because by not accepting what is happening, you are putting your heart in a tug of war much longer than it needs to be.

Shock – At first you may not feel *anything* as you try to wrap your mind around what is happening.

Relapse – You may find yourself going back to

your Ex out of habit. He may even take you back...for sex, or worse, out of sympathy. It may take a while before the relationship is completely over...*to you*. This place of "limbo" is the absolute worst place to be. Some people get stuck in the "breakup-makeup" phase for way too long. They want to keep *trying* to work things out knowing darn well they are in a relationship that's done, finished and has fizzled out. Instead of letting it burn by accepting it and allowing the disappointment to sink in so they can finally move on for good, they let in linger.

Guilt – You may start blaming yourself for the failed relationship and attempt to make things right.

Resentment – Once you accept the breakup and realize that you both will never reunite the way you want to, bitterness starts setting in. You start thinking of all the sacrifices you made and begin resenting the time you "wasted".

Sadness - There are many emotions associated with

a breakup but the universal one is sadness and even depression. It's okay to feel sad because that means that you have accepted it, now that you have accepted it you can start moving on.

Revenge - Sometimes after resentment, a sense of revenge sets in. Some women try to hold his personal belongings hostage, damage his property, some even go as far as revealing his little secrets. Now you want to pour bleach on his clothes, you're listening to Jasmine Sullivan and thinking about "busting the windows out his car". You want to key his truck, fight his new girlfriend...*and if you weren't thinking about doing anything crazy...I hope I didn't give you any ideas.*

Rebound – Not everyone experiences this part of the breakup process, but very many do. It's the gray area where you *think* that you're over your Ex but you're really not. It's when you jump head first into another relationship but you haven't dealt with your feelings associated with your previous relationship. Problems from your suppressed emotions usually arise soon after, and that isn't fair to your new mate.

Letting Go – After going through the previous stages, most people are able to finally let go. After they truly let go of the guilt and resentment some people are actually able to be friends with their Ex's. You may ask yourself: "When is it ever safe to be friends with my Ex?" *Well...let me put it this way,* if he mentions another girl, or you see him with his new girl and you feel absolutely nothing...then it's totally safe. (I wouldn't recommend you testing this out while you're still single though).

Moving on – When you've not only let go, but also moved on, then you're completely over the breakup. Once you're able to open yourself to other people then other people will want to get to know you.

All breakups don't occur in this manner or order. This is just to give you an idea of what is usually expected when someone is going though a breakup.

No one can truly put together a master plan or blue print on how to get over a past relationship within a certain timeframe, however, I interviewed over 30 people who successfully managed to get through their breakups and I'm sure getting advice from others who have been through what you're currently going through will help you to make sense of it all and put you back on track. When I conducted my survey, the most common answer besides prayer was to replace their Ex, not only with someone new, but with someone better. *Realistically, a conversation of closure helps but in the event that closure isn't possible, the results of my survey suggest:*

The quicker you realize you lived before you met him and he was just a mistake, the sooner you'll be able to live life without regrets after him. - CJ

BAJE: Rather than looking at it as a mistake, I'd suggest looking for the lesson in the whole situation. When you see it as a mistake and time wasted that's when resentment sets in, and as long as you're in the 'resentment stage', then it will be harder to move on. So look for the lesson and learn from it so that you're able to move forward.

Transmute the love you had between that person and yourself to a healthy love you have for yourself. Focus on loving you and not needing the love of another. -MN

BAJE: Excellent point, I believe that what's wrong with society today is that since we were children we were taught that we aren't a whole person. So we spend the rest of our lives searching for that **one** person who'll complete us. What if you find that person and then for whatever reason you split, or he passes away, what then? Or even worse, what if you never find that person? Is your whole world going to come crashing down? We need to know that loving ourselves whether or not a mate is in our lives is the foundation of our happiness. If the perfect one happens to come a long, then great! And if he doesn't, then we still have ourselves and we should be happy with that. We as people need to stop setting ourselves up for a life of misery.

Realize that there is always something better than what I had and God will deliver to me who he wants me to be with. -SW

BAJE: Whomever God is to you; you have to believe with all your heart that he will deliver better to you. You may not know when better is coming or where it's coming from but you have to make yourself believe. Hope and faith is what keeps us going.

I look at my pain and realize that my mind creates it by malfunctioning. I move my focus and energy to beautiful and positive things. -DG

BAJE: The mind is a very powerful tool. Once we learn how to focus it we can choose to focus it on positives, rather than negatives.

I upgrade. - FC

BAJE: Simple and straight to the point.

If you love yourself you can get over anything. -BH

BAJE: That's so true, but sometimes people need a little push and encouragement for them to realize their worth.

I get preoccupied with other activities and try to delete all memories of that person out of my mind and anything tactile that reminds me of them. -KL

BAJE: I agree. Get rid of anything that he gave you or anything that reminds you of him if you can. (If it's expensive...sell it). If you both have a sentimental landmark try not to visit the site.

Move on to the next! -EA

BAJE: Life goes on!

Place something else in his or her place; and I thank God for my health and move on. -NR

BAJE: Sometimes we're so wrapped up in our own situation that we fail to realize that so many people are going through much worse. We need to take frequent breaks to be grateful for the things that are going right in our lives.

Keeping faith in God and daily prayer helps to guide me.   -TG

BAJE: Enough said. It's not that prayer always changes things, but it changes our outlook on things and helps us to put things in perspective.

I simply forget that they ever existed. I completely erase them for my mind. -LF

BAJE: Sounds easy, but in reality it's easier said than done.

Move somewhere far; keep busy with work or a hobby. Then I start dating. -OP

BAJE: I wouldn't go as far as moving far but I'd suggest moving out of your current apartment if your finances allow, especially, if you both spent a lot of time there. In the meantime definitely go out and meet other people.

I think about all the bad things that they did in the relationship. -YN

BAJE: If you start missing him then think about all the reasons *why* the relationship didn't work out in the first place. However, you have to be conscious not to become bitter and realize that everyone that you'll meet in the future isn't the person who hurt you in the past.

Get in a zone with something I love to do. -IR

BAJE: I'm all about making 'To Do' lists. Make a list of things that you love to do and pencil them in on your calendar, (scheduling daily activities is a good start).

Surround myself with family and friends and get out of his circle of associates (including children if it will cause me pain). –GS

BAJE: While you're in this phase, it's very important to have people you trust close to you. Don't hesitate to seek them out for advice and moral support. Unfortunately, if your Ex has children that you've grown close to, you're going to have to separate yourself from them. It doesn't have to be abrupt but you must take measures to disconnect gradually. It isn't doing you or the child any good to keep holding on. The quicker you let go is the quicker you can move on.

I stay busy! -PD

<u>BAJE:</u> That's definitely a great start.

Be with people who can make you laugh. : D -SK

<u>BAJE:</u> You definitely want to be around people who are aware of your circumstances and sensitive to the situation. Stay away from cynical and negative people. Surround yourself with friends and family who are uplifting and who'll do things to take your mind off of the current situation. Laughter is truly the best medicine for the spirit.

I keep a journal to keep track and process my thoughts and I also have a few nights of binge drinking. - BC

<u>BAJE:</u> Writing is very therapeutic. It's a great way to track your growth. Months later you'll look at your notes and say, "I can't believe I ever felt like that!"

There is nothing wrong with a drink occasionally, just make sure you don't open up a whole new problem, (alcoholism).

I separate myself from others and I self reflect on what I did in the relationship. What I did that was positive and what was negative. -AH

BAJE: When separating yourself, be careful not to isolate yourself. Self reflection is important because when you not only look on what went wrong on his side, but on your part also, you can work on those things and be better prepared for your future relationships.

Kill them. I'm just joking. -RF

BAJE: Watch out buddy! If there is one thing I learned throughout life, is that there's some truth to every joke.

I tell everyone that it's over between us, so that I'm not tempted to ever re-connect. -TT

BAJE: That's an awesome technique if you feel that you're not yet strong enough to sever the connection.

I drink alcohol, smoke weed and have rough casual sex with strippers. -VN

BAJE: This is all wrong. *It isn't hard to figure out that this advice came from a guy.*

I deal with it myself; other people's opinions will have you all messed up. -CT

BAJE: If those close to you have a tendency to give you advice that does more harm than good, then you're going to have to muster up strength from within to get through this. If that fails then seek out professionals.

I get over a breakup with music. -SH

BAJE: Music has a way of healing the heart. It's a positive way to escape to a happy place at anytime you choose.

Chocolate and ice cream always make me feel better. -OE

BAJE: A little chocolate and ice cream always puts a smile on my face temporarily; but be careful not to overindulge.

Have a nice stiff drink and jump back in the dating thing! *Screw it!* **-JN**

BAJE: It takes courage to jump back in the swing of things, but the quicker you can build up the strength to do so, is the less power that your Ex has over you.

I dedicate time to help a cause to keep my focus away from thinking about my Ex. -HB

BAJE: There are so many people in need who you can dedicate your time to help. Help people who will greatly appreciate you because they know that you're not obligated to help, but you're helping because you really want to. There's The Boys & Girls Club, there is Meals on Wheels (where you can deliver hot meals to seniors) and you can walk for the AIDS Foundation or the American Cancer Society. It's a double win because not only are you helping to raise funds and awareness for a good cause but you'll also get in shape. For a list of non-profit organizations you can volunteer for visit www.MissBaje.com

I find someone better who does all the things that the other loser didn't. -WK

BAJE: I Love it! I couldn't have said it any better.

I go out and date a bunch of cute boys (nothing long-term, just serial dating). Looking great is great revenge. –BT

BAJE: That's a good one. Serial dating is okay as long as you're not looking for anything long-term and as long as you're not having sex with all of these guys. Dressing up and looking your best does wonders for your self-esteem, but don't do it for him...do it for you. Though it is true that while working through a breakup most of us want to sulk and be isolated, this isn't the time to allow your emotions to take over. You have to use logic. The more you're alone is the more you'll think about your current situation. Go out and meet people. You've already spent enough time on your Ex, don't waste another second whining over him. When you're out meeting people, at first you may only stop thinking about him for a few minutes at a time; but the more you interact with people, those minutes become hours and those hours turn into days.

I talk to a good friend. -GA

BAJE: Having someone you can confide in will help to speed up the healing process dramatically. Sometimes it can be a bit difficult speaking to a friend about what you're going through if they haven't been through it themselves because they just can't relate. However, even though they may not have all the answers, just having someone you can vent to will help to take some of the load off of your shoulders.

I don't smell, talk to or see him. It's a chemical called Oxytocin. -PL

BAJE: I honestly must say that I have never heard of this chemical, which led me to do some research. Wikipedia refers to Oxytocin as the "love hormone". Recent studies have begun to investigate its role in various behaviors such as orgasms, social recognition and pair bonding. So ladies, that t-shirt of his that you just love to sleep in...it's time to toss it out.

I stay busy with things in life that build self-esteem like working out. -RD

BAJE: Staying busy is one thing; staying busy with things that make you feel good about yourself is even better. You'll feel better when you take part in activities that make you feel good as a person, like helping others that are less fortunate than you are. Sometimes we think that we are going through hell...until we encounter others that are stuck in hell.

I find another source of happiness in exchange for that loss. -FJ

BAJE: Don't see it as a loss, but rather as a new chapter because there are a lot of lessons to be discovered in your past relationship that you can apply to your new one.

I replace them quickly with what brings me peace and value for myself. Life is too wonderful and feelings change. If you want to make the change then you can do it in 2 to 5 seconds. –AB

BAJE: Don't chase him; replace him.

I work on accomplishing something worthwhile and amazing in my life that I KNOW would make

them and anyone else say "Damn!" -EN

BAJE: That's such an awesome goal!

Become a lesbian. -TD

BAJE: If you like women that's one thing, but don't allow one man to have to power to turn you off from the whole male population. Contrary to popular beliefs, I'd like to think that there are some good men left.

I focus even harder on my work, life and overall success. Victories in my business give me the endorphins I need to feel happy without him and be content all by myself. -WL

BAJE: Well said! Do more of the things that get you going!

I constantly tell myself that there is someone better that I just haven't met yet. -FR

<u>BAJE:</u> That's right; keep hope alive! They say that you can live 40 days without food, 4 days without water, 4 minutes without air, but you can't live 4 seconds without hope.

When I realize I have a void, I find something else to replace that space. -SY

<u>BAJE:</u> Notice that she said 'something' and not necessarily 'someone'; it's just too soon. Find something positive to fill that space.

Love is love. If it hurts then it's not love. You met as friends you should leave as friends. –TC

<u>BAJE:</u> Don't be bitter, be better!

So you see...you are not the first one who has had their heart broken, and you won't be the last. Many people have been where you are now, and they have not only survived, but also thrived. You'll be okay. It's extremely rare for anyone to meet the person that they are completely compatible with the first time around. It's by meeting more of the people that you don't want to be with that makes you recognize the type of person that you do want to be with once they come along. More importantly, know that it's meeting more of the people that you don't want to be with that will make you appreciate the one that you do want to be with when you finally meet him.

THE BREAKUP GUIDE

Chapter 3

I Love Me Too Much!

I Love Me Too Much!

If you have time to mope around and feel sorry for yourself then you have too much time on your hands. I love me too much to sit around the house crying and being depressed! I love me too much to not go out and make new friends! I love me too much to not be happy! The only person right now with the power to make you happy is you...so shake off the blues and make it happen!

Sometimes it's better to start new and stop wasting precious time trying to patch up what was never meant to be in the first place. If you've been trying so hard to fit a piece into a puzzle and it doesn't fit then it just doesn't fit. It's time to come to the realization that it just doesn't belong there.

In a lot of cases, not being able to get over someone has to do with how we truly feel about ourselves on a deeper level. Your self-esteem should have nothing to do with how others feel about you but it should have everything to do with how you feel about *yourself.* When you are confident in yourself, then you know that you will be fine whether or not you are in a relationship. Other people's opinions of you wont affect the way you see yourself. You wont accept just any kind of treatment from anyone; you'll only accept the best.

Take a few minutes to reflect on the positive qualities and great personal traits that you posses. Go on, its okay to bask in all your glory.

What are some things that you do well?

_____

_____

_____

_____

_____

_____

_____

_____

_____

_____

_____

_____

_____

_____

_____

_____

_____

_____

_____

_____

_____

_____

<u>What are some of your accomplishments?</u>

_____
_____
_____
_____
_____
_____
_____
_____
_____
_____
_____
_____
_____
_____
_____
_____
_____
_____
_____
_____
_____
_____

What are some things that make you feel good?

_____

_____

_____

_____

_____

_____

_____

_____

_____

_____

_____

_____

_____

_____

_____

_____

DO THINGS THAT MAKE YOU FEEL GOOD

Before you can start to feel good you have to release the negative energy out. Most people let it out by crying, some by exercising, some by going to the gym or hitting a punching bag and if you're like me then you may choose to *write it out.*

- If it will make you feel better go ahead and write a letter to your Ex just to get out all your thoughts and then rip it into 100 pieces and throw it away. That's right, he'll never get it, this is strictly for you. When you throw that letter away, envision yourself letting go of all the negative feelings; all the hurt, sadness, rejection, bitterness, jealousy, and resentment.

- Throw yourself a pity party. Yes I said it! Cry and let it all out, then all your girls over and talk about the situation, order a pizza and watch a movie with them. You are human, it hurts, you have to vent. *However* this party should only last ONE day; after that its time to start moving forward.

- Stay looking your best...not for him, but for you. If the word gets out about how gorgeous you look and it happens to get back to him, then that's absolutely great! When you look good you'll feel great.

- Accessorize! We women just love ornaments. There is something about bling, sparkles, glitter, glitz and glamour that does something to us! We love earrings, necklaces, anklets, bracelets, rings and anything that glistens. We love purses, sunglasses, hats and especially shoes! I don't know why but we do and oddly enough; these small items boost our confidence and make us feel good about ourselves. (Hey! Whatever works). I'm not suggesting that you go out and spend all your money on these items but go through your closet and get jazzy. Use what you already have to jazz yourself up! So even if today is just an ordinary day and all you're doing is running errands, jazz up that normal tank top and jeans by wearing a pair of sexy heels, a bright blazer and that floral sheer scarf that makes you feel like a boss! Or how about that fancy outfit that you've wanted to wear but haven't had an extravagant event to wear it to? Now is the time to find an extravagant event. Put on that outfit and turn heads. Just put on something that will make you feel alive! Flip through a magazine for ideas; be bold and try something new!

- Get pampered. Go to a nail salon and get a matching manicure & pedicure...make yourself feel pretty, make yourself feel like a lady.

- Pamper yourself. If you're on a budget then give yourself a manicure and pedicure or call one of your girlfriends over and you can do hers and she can do yours.

- Give yourself a relaxing homemade facial. Its okay if you haven't done it before just gather a headband, washcloth, clean towel, box of tissues, facial steamer or pot with water, cleanser, scrub, witch hazel, a mask, cucumber slices or chamomile tea bags (already steeped) and a moisturizer and then look up YouTube videos on: *How to give yourself a facial.*

- Treat yourself to something cute or delicious, but inexpensive; this isn't an excuse to squander money. Something affordable can still put a smile on your face...like flowers, your favorite ice cream or a cupcake from that fancy bakery in town.

- Have a reading date with yourself. Turn off your phone and go to the park, a trendy café or find a comfortable place at home and read something inspirational for an hour or more. Have some hot herbal tea, exotic fruits or cheese & crackers with a glass of wine. Fully enjoy the experience.

- Look up some inspirational videos on the Internet. Some people who I find inspirational are Oprah, Will Smith, Tyler Perry, Tyrese Gibson, Eric Thomas, Les Brown and Tony Robbins. Even look up videos on *How to be Happy* or *How to Get Over a Breakup.* Hearing other people's perspectives and how they worked though their issues may help you tremendously.

- Start smiling!! Right now!! (Don't give me the side eye like I'm some kind of weirdo). I'm serious! Put a smile on your face. It doesn't have to be a big cheesy smile where all of your thirty-two teeth show, just a soft subtle smile. It's almost impossible to think of sad thoughts while there is a smile on your face...that's just not the way our minds are wired. Do your part by putting a smile on your face and your mind will do the rest. Remember, you control your mind, *not* the other way around. By simply smiling you'll gradually get in a better mood. You'll start to remember things that made you smile in the past. You'll seem more inviting to others and you'll open up yourself for positive energy to come your way. Try it!...Now! If it's hard for you to keep a smile on your face then try this. Get a sheet of paper...right now...or open the memo pad in your phone and make a list of things that made you smile or laugh in the past. Keep that list, name it your "happy file" and refer to it any time you need a pick-me-up. Whenever you think of something else that puts a smile on your face just add it to your list. : D

Before I give you advice on some of the things that you should do in order to get over your breakup quicker, I'm going to give you a list of some things that you should not do.

<u>THE LIST OF DONT's</u>

Don't talk to him.

Don't talk about him. (If others bring him up tell them that you rather not bring up the past).

Don't try to make your Ex jealous, it makes you look desperate and bitter...and that's just *not* a good *look*.

Don't spend too much time with mutual friends

who you and your Ex have in common because they'll remind you of him.

Don't be angry. It's a waste of time, especially when it's something that you can't change. Each minute you give into anger is one precious minute you've robbed yourself of happiness!

Don't listen to sad songs or love songs. Even though you may be tempted to listen to sappy songs that match your mood over and over, don't give into it.

Don't spend time reminiscing (that's backwards); you don't want to be stuck in limbo land; limbo land sucks!

Don't stalk him OR his social networks.

Don't throw a public divorce or breakup party. It's not something to be celebrated. Be the bigger person and just move on with your life in a classy manner. (I've seen people design flyers and really go the whole nine yards with this).

Don't try to be friends until you are really, really over him.

Don't use holidays or his birthday as an excuse to call or text him.

Don't do drugs, or indulge in over excessive alcohol in attempt to numb the pain. It's ok to feel, it's how we learn, and more importantly how we grow.

Don't ask anyone who knows him about his new girlfriend. Keep your dignity; you do not need to know.

DON'T 'HOOK' UP WITH YOUR EX...AT ALL!

Don't bad mouth your Ex; try to put yourself in his shoes. If he wasn't happy for whatever reason then he has the right to leave.

Don't be sad. If for no other reason, be happy because you could have been stuck in a one sided relationship much longer and in the long run that hurts even worse.

Don't tell the break-up story to your friends and family over and over. Tell them once & then stop torturing them. It's not their burden to bare. At some point you have to put your big girl panties on.

Don't tell your friends and family of the breakup the first time you breakup because most couples go through the motions of a breakup a few times before they *actually* breakup for real. To make sure that the breakup is official I would advise you to wait until there is about one full week of no communication with your Ex before you start telling anyone. Otherwise you'll seem indecisive to them and even worse, when you really need their moral support they'll feel like you're just going through the motions again.

<u>THE LIST OF DO's</u>

If you believe in prayer, now is the time for it and if you believe in God or a higher power now is the time to call on him. Pray for clarity and strength and for the confusion and pain to go away.

Secondly, erase your Ex's number from your phone so that you won't "drunk dial" him on the nights that you're feeling vulnerable.

The key to getting over someone is to focus on EXACTLY WHY the relationship ended in the first place.

Write down your feelings in a journal (I'll cover more on this later in Chapter 10).

Find a new, exciting hobby.

If you already have a hobby... get a new one.

Ask your friends and parents how they got over their past loves.

If you're feeling angry about the breakup, try some tension releasing exercises like meditation or yoga.

If you're feeling sad about the breakup, try some energy boosting exercises like a dance class or go jogging.

Be a part of something bigger than you. Volunteer for a non-profit organization.

Break your everyday cycle. Do something to jump out of your normal daily routine. Bake a cake, cook a fancy dinner; just do something you normally wouldn't.

Create a strict schedule and stick to it. If you have a lot of free time throughout your day, then schedule an activity in those hours. Each hour of your day should have something specifically scheduled. E.g. After work, schedule yourself to go running from 6pm-7pm. Read a chapter of a book from 7pm-8pm etc.

Do a clean sweep of your home and get rid of all

memorabilia pertaining to your EX.

Clean and organize the area you live and work in. It will make you feel better and make your mind less cluttered. Plus it requires your undivided attention so it will keep your worries at bay.

Start some type of exercise regimen. It will release endorphins that will help to alleviate depression. (Don't be afraid to start small. You don't have to exercise for a whole hour, start with 20 jumping jacks, sit-ups or pushups.

Be Social...and I'm not just talking about online. Go out and meet new people, lots of new people. Use this time to meet new friends, improve relations with old friends and network. A well-balanced life will lessen the impact of a breakup, because you will still have the other aspects of your life intact, and improving. Ps. You do not have to wait for someone else to introduce him or herself to you first. Be bold and initiate conversations with strangers...remember all your friends now were once strangers.

Form a circle of 5 POSITIVE people; people you feel good around, people who make you feel good about yourself and then make it a point to see or talk to at least one of them each day. In this vulnerable time you need as much positive energy around you as possible.

Read or watch something inspirational.

Lie on the beach or by the side of a pool and just relax.

Get a pet. If you may not be ready for a full time pet, then offer to pet-sit for your friends or walk your neighbor's dog. Pets give such unconditional love; they're bound to put you in a better mood…if you're a pet lover.

Have a picnic with friends, or with your pet, or even by yourself.

Watch the news, not often…just a few times; just

enough for you to realize that your problems aren't as bad as they seem compared to people who are starving, sick and dying!

Masturbate...yes I said it! Start doing it and start doing it as often as you need to. After a sexual release you may be able to think more clearly.

Stock the fridge with healthy foods (just in case you go on a food binge)

Your sense of smell is the strongest sense that's linked to your memory. You remember his T-shirt that you used to sleep in, the one that smells like him, the one that comforts you and reminds you of him? Yeah, that one! Go get it right now, smell it one last time, now riiiiiip it! Rip it some more. Now, you may throw it away.

It's okay to cry, just cry to anyone *except* the culprit who's making you cry.

Speak less of him. It's not going to be easy but you have to learn how to change your thoughts from negative to positive "ON PURPOSE". When you hear yourself talking about him immediately stop, flip the switch and talk about something else.

Record yourself on your webcam and just talk about how you're feeling. Sometimes it's not necessarily answers that we need; we just need to express our anger or sadness. Most times it's just that act of venting that starts the heeling process. You don't have to post your videos for anyone else to see. Months later when you review them you'll see just how much you've grown.

Its easy to follow a set plan, the hard part is when you get thrown a curve ball! I'll cover a few.

<u>WHAT IF'S</u>

What if...**you have finally accepted the breakup and you haven't heard from him in weeks and then he calls you out of the blue?**

So what? The last thing you need is someone controlling your emotions. Just think logically. Stay strong and don't be overwhelmed by emotions. Just think about *why* the relationship ended in the first place. You don't have to be rude but just end the conversation.

What if...**he comes back begging?**

So what if he does? Even if you have already forgiven him, would you be able to trust them again? Trust is a very hard thing to win back, even when you can forgive him it's almost impossible to forget.

What if...you've already erased his number from your phone but you still know it by heart? How do you stop yourself from calling him when you are drunk, lonely or feeling vulnerable?

Keep some notes in the memo section of your phone that lists all the bad things he did to you and lastly, the reason why you broke up...then read it again and again before you dial his number. That should help to put your emotions back in check.

What if...you see couples cuddling and making out & you get overly emotional?

There will be some days when your emotions seem overwhelming; like when you are PMS-ing etc. You may feel like bursting into tears, that's ok, just yell to the lovers, "Get a room!" and keep it moving. Your day is coming :)

What if...you find yourself constantly checking his social sites?

To protect you from yourself you can use a software program or browser extension to block you from accessing a certain web pages. (Almost like parental control settings). Google it.

To be certain your Ex doesn't hurt you again or play with your emotions stay away until you're fully over him.

So...how do you know that you're fully over him?

When you can wish him well.

When you hope that he is happy.

When you can see him with a new woman and not be upset.

When you are able to forgive him.

You may not have fully forgiven him but you may be at the point where you can at least pray for him.

<u>BE HONEST WITH YOURSELF</u>

Never look at your past relationship as a waste of time because you'll not only resent your Ex for life but you'll probably resent yourself also. Look at it as a learning experience. It's better to learn the thing you need to know now, rather than later. Besides, I'm sure that at some point, you were happy in the relationship so give thanks that those times did exist.

Now, I'm not saying act like you're not feeling pain; it's actually healthy to allow yourself to feel those emotions too, so you can acknowledge them, deal with them, cry it out and move on. Sweeping the un-addressed pain under the rug can actually cause deeper emotional trauma to you and conflict in future relationships. Deal with it and move on.

Be the bigger person; don't deny it. Don't say you never loved him because you did, that's why you're mad now. Its ok to acknowledge that you love him, and perhaps you always will in some shape or form but you just can't coexist; then move on. Think about how the earth needs the sun to thrive, but if the sun were any closer it would kill all forms of life. Sometimes it just makes more sense to love someone from a distance.

Lesson: #8. *Just because two people love each other doesn't mean that they're meant to be together.*

If you're in a relationship that just isn't working, do not be afraid to end it. Because it ends doesn't mean you're a failure. If the relationship wasn't a healthy one then you're actually a winner.

MOVE ON TO THE NEXT...BUT SLOWLY

You can't worship people; they will let you down at one point or another...it may be with something small or something huge. With every relationship that you form, just know that one day it WILL come to an end…hopefully later than sooner. Sometimes its through a breakup, sometimes you grow apart, if not, then eventually its through death. In most cases you'll get hurt to some degree when that relationship comes to an end, but don't let that stop you from taking the leap of faith again. I've been hurt like we *all* have been. Even though while I was working my way through the 'hurting stage', I said that it's better to not love at all and not have my heart broken; once my heart was mended I was excited to take that leap of love all over again. To live a life of fear is such an awful way to live. After it's all said and done, you can't deny that the fall was full of adrenalin, passion and anticipation, and those are the moments in life worth living for. At the very least, years down the line you can reflect on those brief moments of bliss, smile and say "good times, good times". Some people go through their entire lives and never experienced love on any level. *You will survive fear, you will survive pain…you will survive.*

OTHER BOOKS TO READ TO HELP YOU GET OVER IT

I'm recommending some "breakup" books below; I got them off of http://www.dating.about.com (just in case you need more reading material after this book).

He's Just Not That Into You

It's a classic single-woman scenario: you really like this guy, but he's giving mixed messages. You make excuses; decide he's confused, afraid of commitment. Behrendt, a former executive story editor for Sex and the City—and a formerly single (now happily married) guy who knows all the excuses—provides a simple answer: he's just not that into you. Stop kidding yourself, let go and look for someone else who will be. After all, as Behrendt sensibly puts it, *"if a (sane) guy really likes you, there ain't nothing that's going to get in his way."* If you're not convinced yet, by all means read this smart, funny and surprisingly upbeat little book, full of q's and a's covering every excuse woman has ever made to avoid admitting to herself that a man just wasn't that smitten with her. Copyright © Reed Business Information

It's Called a Breakup because It's Broken

The most modern and laid-back of the top breakup books in this list, "It's Called a Breakup Because Its Broken" was written by the now-famous Sex and the City writer, Greg Behrendt, and his wife Amiira after his previous book, "He's Just Not That Into You" hit the bestsellers list. Although there is little in this book that can't be found elsewhere, Behrendt's fresh style, sometimes crass responses to Dear Abby-like situations and honest reminders that we'll all find love again can be exactly what younger audiences need in order to move past the breakup grieving phase.

The Journey From Abandonment to Healing

For those familiar with Elizabeth Kubler-Ross' "On Death and Dying", this relationship book takes a similar stance, denoting the five stages of grief every human being endures. The differences between the two books are subtle, yet important: Kubler-Ross' book focuses on loss through death, whereas Anderson discusses how the five steps are managed during a relationship breakup. Part science and part real-life exploration, "The Journey from Abandonment to Healing" is a gentle yet informative read that every breakup sufferer should get their hands on.

Getting Past Your Breakup

An excellent breakup book that assists not only in dealing with the shock of a relationship ending, but also how to move past the breakup to become a stronger, better person in spite/because of it. Topics such as dealing with breakup myths ("I need closure!") and boundaries (how do I not get into this situation ever again) are refreshing and well suited to the tone and style.

How to Survive the Loss of a Love

A concise 200-page book full of truisms, proverbs, poems and reminders assisting those who are grieving the loss of a loved one. How To Survive the Loss of a Love doesn't focus exclusively on breakups (it is meant for anyone struggling with relationship loss, whether it be through divorce, illness, death, breakup and so forth) but it does provide solace and support like few other relationship books double its size. With over two million copies in print, this book is an easy read to carry around with you wherever you go, and is perfect to share with a grieving friend once you've finished with it.

Rebuilding When Your Relationship Ends

Although this book is focused on those trying to recover from a divorce, the information shared within is extremely useful to anyone struggling through a particularly difficult breakup. Not only does Rebuilding provide practical tips and suggestions for working through a breakup, it also explains in a fair amount of detail the normal physiological responses one's body goes through while processing a breakup. Interestingly, the book doesn't focus solely on the person who is grieving being broken up with, but covers information for the person breaking up the relationship as well.

How to Heal a Broken Heart in 30 Days

Practical advice given for men and women alike fills this supportive relationship book in a warm, comforting way that many other breakup books lack. Coming from the viewpoint that everyone will suffer from a bad breakup at one point or another in their lives, authors Howard Bronson and Mike Riley don't pull any punches either when it comes to getting down to business and healing after relationship loss.

Eat, Pray, Love

Gilbert (The Last American Man) grafts the structure of romantic fiction upon the inquiries of reporting in this sprawling yet methodical travelogue of soul-searching and self-discovery. Plagued with despair after a nasty divorce, the author, in her early 30s, divides a year equally among three dissimilar countries, exploring her competing urges for earthly delights and divine transcendence. First, pleasure: savoring Italy's buffet of delights--the world's best pizza, free-flowing wine and dashing conversation partners--Gilbert consumes la dolce vita as spiritual succor. "I came to Italy pinched and thin," she writes, but soon fills out in waist and soul. Then, prayer and ascetic rigor: seeking communion with the divine at a sacred ashram in India, Gilbert emulates the ways of yogis in grueling hours of meditation, struggling to still her churning mind. Finally, a balancing act in Bali, where Gilbert tries for equipoise "betwixt and between" realms, studies with a merry medicine man and plunges into a charged love affair. Sustaining a chatty, conspiratorial tone, Gilbert fully engages readers in the year's cultural and emotional tapestry-- conveying rapture with infectious brio, recalling anguish with touching candor--as she details her exotic tableau with history, anecdote and impression. Copyright Reed Business Information

SOME POEMS TO HELP YOU GET OVER IT

Don't Let Him Bring You Down

Don't let him bring you down,

The words he speaks are useless.

Let him suffer emotionally

As you pride yourself in what you have accomplished.

Don't let him bring you down

And drown in his ...own pool of self-pity.

Stand up and remind yourself that you are a strong woman

That doesn't need his negative tongue lashing out at a beautiful day.

Don't let him bring you down,

You deserve what he never gave and could never give.

Look at yourself in the mirror and accept the realization

That you don't need a man,

Not just an ordinary man with mounds of drama taller than himself.

Believe in yourself, and stay true to what you deserve as an independent woman.

Look him the eye, laugh at his words,

Don't shed a tear, for he is not worth it.

Make him swallow his tongue

Regret his poor decisions in his own life of remorse.

You stand there as beautiful as you are

And say, "I don't need you".

And smile your smile,

And walk you walk with more confidence

Than you have ever had before.

-By Michelle Barton.

Everyone Says Love Hurts

Everyone says that love hurts, but that's not true.

Loneliness hurts. Rejection hurts. Everyone confuse

these things with love, but in reality love is the only

thing in this world that covers up all the pain and

makes us feel wonderful again.

- Unknown

I Know I Will Love Again

When you left me

My heart shattered into a million little pieces,

My life crumbled under your feet.

As you walked out that door,

You took my soul with you,

Onto that old cobbled street.

At first I could not accept it,

There was no way that you were gone.

I played this song over and over,

Tomorrow he will come back home.

And tomorrow turned into a million yesterdays,

As my life slowly wilted away.

I became a drooping flower,

Thirsting every day.

But still I could find no water,

For my source it was only one.

And it dried up forever for me,

When your love became undone.

I thought I would die without you,

And I slowly counted the days,

When I would meet my savior,

In a loveless haze.

But the days turned into years,

And still I was on this earth,

Nobody came to save me,

From my loveless hearth.

Then one day I finally realized,

That you were never coming back again.

And as long as I kept hoping for you,

My heart would be in pain.

A broken heart shattered in pieces,

Can never love again.

So I opened up my door,

And I stepped gingerly onto that old street.

Walking down that path to love

So scary and yet oh so sweet.

-By Injete Chesoni.

Love?

When love has come

But soon is gone

It begs the question

Was it there?

The love was lost

And never found

Lost without you

Lost without me

Lost into eternity

The love was just a figment

A figment of our minds

Something we could ponder

But never express

Was it love or just a feeling?

Was it love or just healing

Healing from the hatred

The hatred of our hearts

Our past was deep and full of pain

We needed this to release the stain

For this I do not regret

The time with you that I had spent

-By Gary R. Hess

PLAY LIST

I'll share with you some of my personal favorite songs that got me through some of my roughest times, perhaps they'll help you out also. I'd recommend that you make a playlist and listen to it on the days that you're feeling down the most.

I'd suggest even falling asleep to the playlist you created because the last thing on your mind is more than likely what you'll dream about all night. So fall asleep to some motivational and "feel good" music.

There are even comedic radio stations that play nothing but comedians delivering stand up jokes. Set your radio to one of those stations for a day. While you're in your car driving around town it will take your mind off of the sad thoughts and put you in a better mood.

<u>FEEL GOOD PLAYLIST</u>

"Not Gonna Cry" – Mary j Blige

"Me, Myself and I" – Beyonce

"I Just Want It to Be Over" – Keisha Cole

"Let it Burn" – Usher

"Stay" - Sugarland

"No Woman No Cry" –Bob Marley

"I Can See Clearly Now" – Jimmy Cliff

"Don't Worry, Be Happy" – Bobby McFerrin

"Survivor" – Destiny's Child

"Irreplaceable" – Beyonce

"Single Again" – Trina

"I Don't Want You Back" - Eamon

"Fighter" – Christina Aguliera

"Listen" – Beyonce

"No More Pain" – Mary j Blige

"99 Problems" – Jay Z

"Stronger" – Kelly Clarkson

"I will Survive" - Gloria   Gaynor

Notice that the songs go from "regret" to 'I'm glad I'm over you'. I don't want to deprive you of wallowing, you can cry if you need to for the first four songs but after that get over it already so we can move on to the empowering songs & empowerment feelings.

HARSH BUT TRUE

If a guy breaks up with you, it's best for you to just move on and try your best to forget about him, and here is why. Even if he takes you back it's highly unlikely that the doubts or problems that were originally lingering are going to disappear with one conversation. Often times people who've broken up once…keep breaking up and that is such an unhealthy way to live. When he tells you that he wants to breakup, trust that he means what he is saying. If you plead for him to take you back and he actually does, just know that you're only keeping the bench warm until whomever he really wants comes his way.

Sometimes it's better to start new and stop wasting precious time by trying to patch up what was never meant to be from the start. If you've been trying so hard to fit the pieces of the puzzle together and it just doesn't fit, its time to come to the realization that it just doesn't belong there. Besides, as long as you're hoping that he'll come back, you are keeping the door closed for your blessings and for great people to enter your life.

You can and WILL find better, but you have to let go of him first (tell yourself this everyday until you actually start to believe it). Love isn't one sided; you deserve to be loved by someone with the same intensity that you love them. Don't be a "convenience". You deserve to be appreciated and not just tolerated.

You can't allow one little guy to make your self-esteem or self-love plummet. He is only one man. Stop acting like there aren't a few million of them in this world. Which leads me to one of the simple but profound things that my father told me about dealing with a man: "There are two things you should never chase behind...a bus and a man".

If you can stop thinking emotionally and start thinking logically for just a moment, you'll realize that all the time you are using to whine over this guy is the same time you can be doing something life changing for yourself! Stop saying you "cant" get over it, because you can!

THE BREAKUP GUIDE

Chapter 4

30 Days to Happiness

<u>30 Days to Happiness</u>

If you want to record videos or keep a journal about how you feel each day, or about how you feel about each of the daily activities that I'm suggesting to you, that would be great. Remember that you don't have to post the videos online, and you can destroy the journal when you're finished. This exercise is just to get you in touch with your feelings. By getting all your thoughts and feelings out, you may be able to create some closure.

<u>Day 1: Take a Freebie</u>

Sulk, sob, wallow, cry, whine, weep, complain, kick and scream...then drag your behind to bed because when the dawn rolls in I don't want you to shed one more tear. You get one day and one day only to get it all out so take advantage of it. Tell the empty room a piece of your mind like your Ex was right there in front of you. Soak the pillows with your salty tears, roll around on the floor like a baby, yell at the top of your lungs...then hush it up and go to sleep. Tomorrow is a brand new day!

Day 2: Turn Up The Music

I know it feels like life kind of sucks, ok...well, life does suck right now BUT it's going get better. Music will help to bring your life back. Music has a great influence on our thoughts and our mood, so turn it up! Select some *feel good* songs and just let your play list flow. Turn up the stereo as loud as your neighbors will allow or hop in your car and go for a ride with the music turned up high or take out your IPod and go for a walk around the block. I promise you that you'll begin to feel the difference.

Day 3: Air His Laundry

Write down all the things that he did wrong, all the things you didn't like about him, and all the times he lied, and cheated and hurt you. Now is not the time to be nice or stingy. If you've run out of paper feel free to get more. When you're finished, write down all the reasons why you deserve better.

Day 4: Do Some Spring Cleaning

Today you need to get rid of everything that you possibly can that reminds you of him. Photographs, trinkets & any other memorabilia and turn in the gifts for some cash. You probably always wanted to have a garage sale, well...now is the time! Then do the ultimate: *Un-friend* him on Facebook, *Un-follow* him on Twitter and delete AND block his phone number AND e-mail address once and for all.

Day 5: Have a Block Buster Night

Order or rent some movies (only comedies! definitely no romance or chick flicks). You can watch them by yourself or invite some friends over for a relaxed fun filled evening. I'd suggested watching the whole season of *America's Funniest Home Videos*. It will have you laughing so hard you'll be holding your stomach and rolling on the floor. As a last resort you can surf the Internet for some funny videos on YouTube.

Day 6: Make a Play List

Make your own playlist of songs that make you feel empowered, songs that make you feel good, free, optimistic, enthusiastic and strong and play them over and over and over.

Day 7: Ride Solo

This evening you're going to get all dolled up, buy yourself a cute (but affordable) dress, go to a makeup counter and get a mini makeover, because tonight you're going out…by yourself! Yeah, that's right, by yourself. You need to get over the myth that you need someone to complete you. You need to get over your fear of being alone. Sure a mate would be *nice* but you are all you *need.* You don't have to wait until one of your girlfriends are available to go out with you and you don't have to wait until you get an invite to go somewhere, just go! Have some trust in yourself; you'll be just fine. Pick a nice lounge around happy hour, smile and don't be afraid to start conversations.

Day 8: Get a New Hair-do

Nothing says 'a new you' like a new 'do'. Try a new hair-do. It can be a different cut, color or style. The compliments and attention you'll get from your friends and co-workers will be sure to boost your self-image.

Day 9: Pamper Yourself

Pampering yourself doesn't have to be expensive. Run a hot bubble bath and relax in it while you sip on hot tea or on a glass of wine. Let the stress and sadness melt away in the water while Beethoven or Mozart plays in the background.

Day 10: Throw Yourself a Curveball

Do something that you normally wouldn't do. Bake a cake, buy a blank canvas at your local art supply store and paint an abstract work of art. Walk your neighbor's dog, offer to babysit your nieces or nephews, go jogging, buy a trivia board game and play it with your family, play some games online; just do something different to take a break from your ordinary schedule.

Day 12: Get Some Air

Get out of the same daily routine. Shake it up a little, take an alternate route home; see some new faces. Today go to a local coffee shop and read a good book or browse through some magazines. If you're not a big coffee drinker, try a smoothie or some steamed milk with a spoonful of sugar.

Day 13: Find Lost Connections

Look up high school and college friends. Try and reach out to past work colleges. Rekindle old flames. Call grandma or other family members that you haven't spoken to in a while. If they don't live too far make a batch of cookies and drop by with them.

Day 14: Give Yourself Credit

What are you good at? Make a list of 20 things that you do well. If more than one person has told you that you're good at something (even if you don't think so), you're allowed to jot that down also.

Day 15: Do Something with a Group of Friends

Round up all your friends and go out in a group. Being with a large group of people you love can be fun. Go to a Comedy club, a jazz show, a fair, a festival, a concert, to dinner, go out for ice cream, or visit an art gallery. It will take your mind off things and remind you that you don't have to be in a relationship in order to smile, laugh or just have fun.

Day 16: Get in Tune with Yourself

Practicing Yoga is not only great for your body but it's excellent for your mind. The meditating aspect of it helps you to focus; it calms your mind and quiets your thoughts. I really started looking more into yoga after I read Russell Simmons' book: *Super Rich.* Mediating will help you to relax. It puts things in perspective and helps you to live life in the present. Try not to dwell on yesterday or worry about tomorrow, just appreciate life now.

Day 17: Get Crafty

Doing things that actually require your concentration will help to distract your mind from the matter at hand. Go to your local art store and pick up some supplies. This year instead of buying gifts for your friends and family members, make something for them. Not only will it save you money, they'll probably appreciate it more because you took the time out to create it. You can buy charms and beads and make them jewelry. You can make a scrapbook and fill it with photos of you and the family, or you can even design your own picture frames.

Day 18: Read a Great Book

Curl up by your fireplace, spread a blanket in a park or just find a quiet spot at home and read a good book. If you're not big on reading then listen to an audio cd. If you're concentrating on reading or listening to something then you're not wasting time thinking about your Ex. I'd suggest self-help books, because not only are you being entertained, you're actually learning practical information you can use to better yourself and sharpen your skills

Day 19: Get Physical

I can not stress this enough! Do something to come out of your slumber. Like *exercise!* Now is the time to get your adrenalin pumping and your blood flowing; I know you don't feel like it...but it's the times that your body doesn't feel like it, that you need to exercise the most. You can hire a personal trainer so you have someone to hold you accountable for working. Even if you are already in good physical shape it doesn't hurt to do some cardio; it will put you in a more positive mental state. You can sign up for a gym membership and set aside a few days each week for you and one of your friends to workout together. If you don't have any friends willing to workout with you this is your chance to meet new friends at the gym.

You can also sign up for an active class like boxing, kickboxing, karate or a Hip Hop, Salsa or ballroom dancing. Just search the Internet for some classes in your area; some colleges also these activities.

If you are on a tight budget and can't afford a gym membership or to sign up for a class then buy a workout DVD or rent one from your local library. If you're on an even tighter budget you can just search for workout or dance videos on YouTube and follow along. Put on some comfortable clothes and make your own living room your gym or dance floor. Get creative and dress the part. Get a full-length mirror so you can see yourself in action and videotape yourself with your webcam so you can watch yourself later.

If you aren't accustomed to working out you'll probably feel like you are going to die...but you won't. Soon your body will get acclimated to it and after each workout you'll feel a boost of energy and will be glad you stuck with it.

Day 20: Open Your Eyes

Do something to open your eyes. See just how big the world is and realize there is so much more out there. Lie out in the backyard and gaze at the stars, look at the sky through a telescope. Go hiking up a canyon; go on the rooftop of one of the highest buildings in your area and just overlook the city. There are millions of people to meet and millions of things to do...start mingling.

Day 21: Just Do Something!

Do something with or without friends. Just get out of the house and do something of your choice. (Exercise your decision-making skills). If you just stay home in bed watching TV...you've failed the test and you're just making things worse on yourself.

Day 22: Make Your Rules

Make a list of things you will and will NOT do. You may feel strong now, but tomorrow you may not feel that strength. So right down your rules now while you can think clearly.

- If you've had a few drinks and you feel like "drunk dialing" or "drunk texting", have a look at your rules.

- If he does happen to call you and you're tempted to accept his call, look at your rules.

- If you're thinking about popping up at his home, work place or favorite hangout spot, look at your rules.

- If you're thinking about posting a message about your breakup on Facebook...you get the point.

Your list should serve as a reminder to stay strong in those moments when you're feeling week.

For example: I will not call him, if he calls I will not answer. If he leaves a voice message I will erase it without listening to it...and so on.

Day 23: Get Sporty

Even if it's something less intense like air hockey or Ping-Pong; just doing something routinely to keep your mind and body active is healthy.

Day 24: Make Love to An Instrument

Learning to play a musical instrument takes a lot of thought, and if you're thinking about playing, then you're not thinking about him. The violin, harp and piano are all sexy instruments.

Day 25: Walk For a Cause

There are so many people battling so many things that are so much worse than a breakup; like Cancer, AIDS, Diabetes and Autism. There are millions of people in a battle simply to stay alive! Consider participating in one of the walks for one of these foundations. You'll meet tons of inspirational people that you can draw strength from, and you'll realize that even though what you're going through sucks...it could suck a lot worse. Here's your chance to make a difference in the life of millions.

Day 26: Get Competitive

Enter a Competition. Do something different and challenging. Enter a pageant; enter a debating competition or even a pie-eating contest. What ever it is that you're good at, chances are there's a competition out there for it. Google it and sign up. The excitement and time you'll use for preparation will be a perfect distraction. Get your family involved too; if they don't want to compete they'll probably come out anyway for moral support. It'll will be fun!

Day 27: Flirt With Yourself

This may sound a bit *cheesy* but it will make you feel better. Look in the mirror and admire yourself. You are beautiful, you are strong, and you are a survivor. Stand up tall, hold your head high, take a deep breath, smile at your reflection and repeat: *"I am beautiful, I am strong, I am a survivor"*. At first you may not believe it but you must keep saying it. Repeat it over and over; say it in your mind, say it in a whisper or say it out loud. However you say it is fine, just say it. Make it apart of your everyday routine: when you're washing your face, brushing your teeth or applying your make up…say it.

Day 28: Make a Bucket List

Make a bucket list of some exciting things that you want to do before you kick the bucket. Ride a roller coaster, swim with dolphins, take a helicopter ride over the city, go sky diving, go to a karaoke bar, go bungee jumping, go skiing, go fishing, take a road trip, play laser tag, shoot some paint ball, go to the gun range, drive a racecar or go scuba diving. The most important part of this exercise is that you actually take the first step to make it happen. Call and inquire about one of these services or also look it up on the Internet and print out some info on it. *Today* take some tome to schedule a day for one of these activities in the near future.

Day 29: Sign up For a Class

Perhaps there is a skill or a trade that you always wanted to learn; use this time to learn it. Use this time to truly become a better version of you.

Day 30: Let It Go

Let it all go. I know this sounds crazy, but you have to forgive him. You have to let go of the anger and resentment otherwise you give him power over you, your future decisions and a huge part of your life. By accepting that your Ex has his *own* set of problems to deal with, your anger will be replaced with understanding. Pray for him. Even in twelve-step programs they tell you to pray for people whom you resent deeply. So forgive him for what he did...and what he failed to do as well.

You can't let all the men you're going to meet pay for his mistakes. You need to live your life fully and freely; you owe that much to yourself. You can't live life fully if you're guarded and you can't find Mr. Right if you're guarded. Your Ex already made you miss out on a lot, don't allow him to make you miss out meeting and falling in love with someone who deserves you and someone who can truly *add* to your happiness.

Just don't forget the lessons from your past relationship and proceed with caution.

THE BREAKUP GUIDE

Chapter 5

Get it Together

Get it Together

So its day three, you're still in bed, haven't showered in days and you look a mess! Get yourself together! Some days you won't know up from down, you wont know if you're coming or going, but life must go on. You still have to go to work, school, the supermarket and take care of your responsibilities. Always have a to-do list on hand and in your short moments of clarity jot down the things that you need to get done. It will help you get through the days where you aren't able to think clearly. The one thing that you don't want to do is to do nothing. Because when your mind is at rest you WILL think of your Ex...so stay busy and tackle that to-do list! When you are back to your normal self you'll be glad that you didn't waste more of your precious time.

Being single isn't the end of the world. You have to realize that having a mate you can get along with and love is great BUT if   that ideal person doesn't come along then you'll *still* be okay! When you truly love yourself regardless of the mistakes you've made, then you'll have a whole new outlook on life.

I don't view being single as a bad thing like a lot of women do. There are a lot of things that women need to work on as individuals before they are able to compliment or complete someone else (like hygiene, patience, jealousy, etiquette, education, career, finances, cooking & home making skills, to list a few). It takes more than attraction and chemistry to make a relationship withstand trials. Embrace that and make a conscious decision to not seek out a relationship until you know that you are fully ready...because when you do get into one, the goal should be for it to last.

It's easy to feel pressured into a relationship from your family, friends, TV, blogs, magazines and society in general, but you have to do it when it feels right for you. Don't just accept any man because everyone around you has a man. Everyone around you may be in a relationship...but that doesn't mean that it's a *happy* relationship. You have *no* idea what goes on behind closed doors. Ignore the pressure. Find a mate when you're ready, in the mean time work on you. Besides...men are more attracted to women who have their stuff together, who know who they are and who don't come off as desperate. So take your time honey...there will never be a shortage of men...ever.

Lesson: #9. Don't chase him, replace him.

Make a list of all the qualities and attributes that you want your ideal mate to possess. Like being:

Romantic, generous, respectful, passionate, supportive, hard working, determined, goal oriented, spontaneous, caring, family oriented, stable, talented, honest, positive, motivated, secure, patient, gentle, intelligent, a non-smoker, well-groomed or affectionate.

Your list can be as long or as short as you want; tailor it to fit you. Once you know exactly what kind of man you want, it will be easier to attract that kind of person.

BREAKUP QUOTES

"If he's dumb enough to walk away, be smart enough to let him go." **– Unknown**

"Letting go doesn't mean giving up... it means moving on." **– Unknown**

"Don't compromise yourself. You are all you've got." **- Janice Joplin**

"Good judgment comes from experience, and often experience comes from bad judgment."

-Rita Mae Brown

"Often the thought of pain is actually worse than the pain itself." **– Unknown**

"Never make someone a priority if they consider you only an option." **– Unknown**

"Life is not about waiting for the storms to pass…It's about learning how to dance in the rain." **- Vivian Greene**

"If I wanted so much to be with the wrong person, how beautiful it will be when the right one comes along." **– Unknown**

"No man is worth your tears and the one that is

won't make you cry." **– Unknown**

"I don't miss him, I miss who I thought he was."

– Unknown

"Life is not the way it's supposed to be. It's the way it is. The way you deal with it is what makes the difference." **- Virginia Satir**

"We sometimes go out of our way to hold on to the wrong one, while we let the right one slip right through our fingers." **– Unknown**

"For few, love can last a lifetime, but for many not knowing when to let go can hold them back forever." **– Unknown**

"Tis better to have loved and lost than never to have loved at all". **– Alfred Lord Tennyson's**

The thing about happiness is that it doesn't help you to grow; only unhappiness does that.

-Lana Turner

"There came a time when the risk to remain tight in the bud was more painful than the risk it took to blossom". **- Anais Nin**

"It is not the strongest of the species that survives, nor the most intelligent that survives. It is the one that is the most adaptable to change."

-Charles Darwin

"It is the friends you can call at 4a.m. who matter."

-Marlene Dietrich

"If you can't save the relationship, then at least save your pride." **– Unknown**

"Although the world is full of suffering, it is also full of the overcoming of it." **- Helen Keller**

"If you can't change your fate, change your attitude." **- Amy Tan**

"If someone you love hurts you, cry a river, build a bridge, and get over it" **– Unknown**

"Relationships are like glass. Sometimes it's better to leave them broken than try to hurt yourself putting it back together." **– Unknown**

"Some people think that it's holding on that makes one strong, but sometimes its letting go."

- **Unknown**

"Pain is inevitable, suffering is optional."

– M. Kathleen Casey

"Love is an adventure and adventure alone is totally worth the risk". **–Baje Fletcher**

LIFE IS ALL ABOUT CHOICES, CHOOSE TO WIN

Trust that this is the best possible thing to happen to you right now, and the reasons will become clearer in the future. Trust God, trust the universe, and trust life. You attract what you think of, so choose to always see the best in any situation life throws your way.

How a man feels about you or how anyone feels about you for that matter should have nothing to do with how you should feel about yourself. As far as your self-esteem goes...how anyone else feels about you is none of your business. Don't let anyone's opinion of you allow you to feel differently about yourself.

Once you know what your value is, you wont ever allow anyone to talk down to you or try to tear you down emotionally, and if they do try then you know that what they say is a mere reflection of themselves and has absolutely nothing to do with you.

Think about some of the things that you are thankful for and take a few moments now to truly feel appreciation for all of those things. The positive feeling of appreciation will put you in a better mood and open the path for more positive energy to flow your way.

So many women loose themselves when they are in relationships. They stop doing what lights them up in an effort to try and please their mates and before you know it, the spark that they once had diminishes. They neglect their friends, their hobbies, their dreams, careers and the goals they once had.

You have to find your identity and know yourself before you can be in a healthy relationship. Know who you are. Your identity and self worth should not ever be defined by *any* relationship, because if it is and that relationship ends then you'll be completely lost. You have to know what you like and dislike and what you want for yourself because you cant expect anyone else to give you what you need in a relationship. Besides, you can't be someone else's half if you're not even a complete half on your own.

Think about what you want now, think about what you always wanted before you were all wrapped up in him and go after it. It's not too late. Men are attracted to women with hobbies, goals and lives of their own...so get one.

THE BREAKUP GUIDE

Chapter 6

When the shoe is on the other foot

When the shoe is on the other foot

Lesson: #10. Sometimes the best thing for you to do…is the hardest thing to do…but you have to do what's right.

It doesn't matter if you are on the receiving or the giving end of a breakup, its tough. I know this because at some point or another I've been on both ends and having to breakup with someone you care about hurts just as bad as being broken up with.

Even though it hurts, most times breakups are absolutely necessary. Nothing lasts forever; good or bad, change is apart of life that we all must adjust to. And believe it or not, change *is* necessary for growth. We cross paths with people for a reason, a season and less often a lifetime. The hardest part of meeting people is knowing *which* people fall into *which* category and *when* that relationship has

146

come to, or needs to come to an end.

PEOPLE GROW AT DIFFERENT RATES

Let me share one of my personal experiences with you. I recall a relationship when I was in my early 20's. I met a guy and he was a good person, he was good to me and we got along. At the time I just started my career as a model and he was pursuing his dream of photography. He encouraged me to start my own modeling agency and I did. We had plans of being a power couple in the entertainment industry. The goal was for me to run the affairs of the agency and for him to do the photography. It seemed like the perfect partnership...on paper, but in real life it was another story. We were to *completely* different people.

When I create a goal I zone in on it. Before you know it I was spending ten hours a day on the computer conducting research, sending out e-mails, making phone calls, looking for new talent, reaching out to casting directors, and building my website.

The woman he first started dating had changed and changed rapidly. He was working a nine-to-five job at the time and he was accustomed to coming home to a home-cooked meal and everything in the house would be tidy and organized...that wasn't so anymore.

He'd go to work for eight hours each day and when he came back and I'd be in the same exact spot that he left me in...dishes still in the sink, no food on the stove and papers everywhere. If I got a call for a last minute audition I would rush and leave town. As you can imagine my new career eventually took a toll on our relationship. The excitement of building my own business became more gratifying than our relationship and our partnership ran its course quickly.

The problem with the relationship was that I thought that we would be putting in the same effort toward our vision and we'd be working at the same pace. But I realized that I wanted to be successful way more and way faster than he did. I was willing to make the sacrifices and go full speed ahead but he preferred the safe approach at a slow and steady pace. None of us were wrong, it was just a matter of preference but I grew faster than he did and the relationship suffered because of it...and that was okay with me because at that point my focus was now on my career.

It wasn't easy calling it off because he really didn't do anything wrong to me and I didn't want to hurt him. He was a genuinely nice guy; he was respectful and caring and I'm sure he'd make a good husband one day...just not mine. I wasn't looking for just a husband, a mate or a nice guy...I needed a partner, a partner that was able to keep up and one I could build an empire with. In my heart I knew that it wasn't going to be him, so the right thing to do was leave, and I did.

<u>LEARN TO RECOGNIZE DYSFUNCTION</u>

Fast forward years later and another guy came in my life like a whirlwind! He was charming, spontaneous and unique. He was just the breath of fresh air I needed. All I wanted to do was laugh and he definitely kept me laughing. He came in my life about a month after I had a terrible tragedy in my family and I just wasn't myself. I was angry, sad and withdrawn, it was a period of vulnerability and for days at a time I just stayed in the house. *(Looking back, here were signs that I see now that if I were in my right frame of mind I wouldn't have ignored).* There were two sides of him. One was romantic, passionate, intimate, helpful and generous while the other side was manipulative, jealous, controlling, condescending and very aggressive. There were many highs but there were even more lows...the true definition of dysfunctional. Reading Tyrese's book: *How to Get out of Your Own Way* helped me not only to recognize dysfunction, but also know what to call it and how to separate myself from it and be totally okay with that decision. So many of us are so messed up in the head that we easily confuse dysfunction with love. I'm regrettably admitting that I used to be one of those people, but today I can proudly say: not anymore.

The relationship became so dysfunctional so quickly. He'd run in front of my car when I tried to leave and would chase the car as I drove away. He'd go through my phone contacts and call & e-mail people without me knowing. There'd be name calling between us, threats as well as threats that were carried out; there'd be fights both verbal and physical. Don't get me wrong just because I knew that ending the relationship was the right thing to do, DID NOT mean that it made it the least bit easier to do so. It was one of the hardest things I had to do. When he cried on the phone and it took him one whole minute for the words "I want to come back home" to ooze out because he was crying so hard...I melted inside. I felt like a mother kicking her only child out of the house. It wasn't easy when he gave me   the 'puppy dog eyes" and begged. He made all kind of promises but I had to block all of that out. I had to dig deep and remember the strength that my grandmother instilled in me. I had to think of all the people over the years who made sacrifices so that I could live a better life. I had to remember all of the sacrifices that I myself made so far. I had to remember all the women who slept on my couch because I had to take them out of their abusive households. Images of Annie, Joan, Mimi, Lisa & Marsha flashed in my mind; It was time for me to start taking my own advice. More importantly, I had to think about my nieces and cousins and all the younger females in my family who looked up to me. Yes I grew to truly care about this guy, but what kind of example was I setting and what kind of message was I sending if I stayed? It took me longer than I should have for me to leave...but the most important thing is that *I left*. Though I knew it was the right decision a huge part of me missed him (the part of him that was romantic, passionate and attentive anyway). But with each day it got easier; it got easier because I got stronger. It also helped tremendously to talk to and be around my true friends. At first I was embarrassed to share with my close friends what I was going through but when I did, they didn't cast judgment and they even shared their past bad relationship stories with me and how they overcame them; and that gave me more strength to overcome mine.

Looking back I can not believe that I accepted that and allowed that type of negativity and dysfunction to seep into my life. It was hard to bring it all to an end because he would just not take "NO" for an answer. Sometimes dysfunction comes with a younger guy or an older man. Sometimes it comes wrapped in pretty little boxes with pretty little bows. Sometimes it comes with a shiny diamond ring...but it's still d-y-s-f-u-n-c-t-i-o-n.

You can shorten the length of the pain caused by a breakup by ending it the minute that you realize that it's just not going to work.

It's not easy. But you CAN force yourself to think logically and not emotionally. Weigh out the pros and cons; and after you do, if all you're left with is..."but I love him"...then it's not going to work. Sometimes love just isn't enough.

If you're in a relationship with someone because you feel sorry for them...it's not going to work. A healthy relationship should be fueled off love and excitement and not off guilt and pity.

If you're in a relationship with someone only because the sex is great...it's not going to work. It takes more than physical intimacy to build a healthy and lasting relationship...it takes things like trust and communication.

If you're in a relationship with someone because of how the person looks...it's not going to work. Remember that looks fade with age. And if the person got in a bad accident their looks can be taken away just like that.

If you're in a relationship only because of what he can do for you financially...it's not going to work. That's like having a leash around your neck and you'll never be able to reach your full potential if you know that the person will always be there to bail you out financially. What if he runs out of money or what if he abruptly cuts you off?

If you're in a relationship because you're scared of the repercussions from your mate if you leave...it's not going to work. If you're that terrified then chances are that he has already threatened you and probably already acted out on some of those threats. *Honey, living in fear is no way to live; actually, living in fear isn't living at all.* Pack up and move if you have to. Get the law involved and inform your friends and family of what's going on. Have them reach out to your abuser because it's your silence that's contributing to his power over you. Once most abusers are exposed or confronted and they know that others know about the situation, they *begin to retract. Their power lies in you not telling anyone so that's why they threaten to do more harm if you do tell. Honey! Tell, tell, tell! Tell anyone who will listen...even if it's a stranger. Someone will extend their hand to help you leave. You can always Google a church, domestic abuse hotline or a shelter for help.*

If you stay in a relationship just because you already have children with your mate...it's not going to work. I think using children as an excuse to stay in a relationship is so wrong. Yes, ideally it's great to have both parents in the household but if it's a household full of dysfunction then it's doing the children more emotional harm than good.

Chapter 7

Finding Courage & Closure

Finding Courage & Closure

I understand what you are feeling because I've been there. It may feel like your world is crashing, you aren't thinking clearly, you may be confused and feel mentally paralyzed...

The un-sugar coated truth: it's a horrible place to be in...but the good news is: that this isn't the end of you; it's a process you just have to work through. Breakups are a normal part of life. It's the end of one thing and the beginning of something ten times better. A breakup simply means that you got all the lessons that you needed from one relationship and its now time to move on to a bigger, healthier relationship; one that will stretch you and help you grow even more. Instead of sulking, live in a place of appreciation. Appreciate the times when things were good, remember the lessons you learned from the situation, let go of the anger, resentment and negative feelings so you can open yourself for the greater things that lie ahead for you.

Lesson #11. We can learn something from each and every person who we encounter.

There are lessons hidden in each relationship; its up to you to uncover them then make the decision to proceed with caution or to not move forward at all.

The sad fact is that most relationships don't last forever. You have to make a conscious effort to cherish the times when things are going well. People change, not everyone you date is the person with whom you will spend the rest of your life with. I'm not even sure if people are meant to spend their entire lives with one single person. Forever is a very long time and not everyone will make that cut. Unfortunately to get to someone with whom you are compatible, you have to date some people with whom you AREN'T compatible with in order to know and appreciate the difference. The great news is that even if most of those relationships don't work, the adversity teaches you and strengthens your character.

THE PARADIGM SHIFT

As hard as it may be try to put yourself in your Ex's shoes, you have to try to see things from his angle. If you just write him off as a *jerk*, you'll miss out on what life is trying to teach you through the relationship.

It may be a personality trait that you need to change,

It may be how to recognize when a relationship is headed for destruction,

It may be how to recognize *when* a relationship is over,

It may be how to stop making excuses for your

mate,

Or it may be what type of men to avoid,

Before you move on to a new relationship take this time to reflect on your old one and see what *you* could have done differently or what *you* could have avoided if you only paid attention.

CREATING COURAGE

So, you may be asking where do you find strength when you can hardly find strength to stand? You already have it! It's within you. You just have to reach inside…and then reach deeper. We all have a reservoir of strength hidden deep inside of us, but in most cases, it's adversity that is able to bring it out. You know what you have to do, and that's *move on*. Now you have to muster the strength to do it. Find courage to close this door of sadness and anger and keep it locked.

If you still feel like you still can't find enough strength from within you, then you can draw strength from your children, your parents, your hobbies, your goals or even your career. When things aren't going according to plan, it seem so much easier to just give in and let depression have its way with us. But it's in these moments where winners are born and losers subside...and you are no looser! The fact that you took the time to read this book proves that you want better for yourself and that is definitely the quality of a WINNER.

CREATING CLOSURE

People are entitled to love whomever they want to love...and if the person they want to love isn't you, you have to be okay with that. People should be able to exercise their power of choice. People grow and people change...as they should. The problem in relationships is when one person makes positive changes while the other makes negative changes; or both my simply head in opposite directions.

Sometimes closure isn't so much as communicating your thoughts to that person as it is just communicating period. Over the years writing worked for me. I wrote down all that I wanted to say to that person both good and bad. The times when I felt vulnerable, or sad or angry I just wrote. The more I filled each page with words, was the better I felt...if only for a moment. Eventually I got tired of writing, (about him anyway) it wasn't until I grew tired of writing that it clicked in my mind; one day it made sense. There were pages and pages of thoughts all about that person; I came to an astonishing realization. Suddenly I associated those "pages" with "time", all those pages were precious time that I spent sobbing over someone who wasn't a part of my life any more, someone who didn't want me, or someone who didn't deserve me; It was time to let go. There was so much I could have been doing instead of wallowing in those emotions. Seeing my time on something tangible like paper helped me to understand that.

Months later when I looked back on all the

things I wrote, I thought, "What was I thinking?!" Sometimes our emotions tend to blow things out of proportion. It isn't until we're back in our right state of mind that we look back and laugh. When you're going through a breakup the hardest thing is looking at the bigger picture and onward to the future. We tend to allow ourselves to be consumed by the situation at hand. Push yourself to picture the future that you want and the future that you deserve.

YOU ARE THE MASTER OF YOUR MIND

One thing I want you to always remember is that if you rely on someone else to make you happy, remember that person also has the power to make you sad. Keep your power. Don't hand over the key to your emotions to anyone. You are the creator of

your life and the master of your future.

Have you ever wondered why sometimes even

though you get a full night's sleep you still wake up feeling drained or even in a bad mood? It is especially important to control what you think about before you go to bed because that is the same emotion your mind will hold onto for the whole time you're asleep.

On the days when you don't feel positive you have to fool yourself, trick your brain, fill your brain with positive things that you *want* to think of rather than the negative things that your brain is automatically thinking. You are the master of your mind, not the other way around. The memories will still be there but will eventually fade into the past with those associated feelings but you have to command the negative thoughts to go away and consciously make an effort to think only positive thoughts. When your mind automatically thinks of something negative, consciously switch into the positive lane.

YOU DESERVE A FAIR SHOT AT LOVE

I can look you in the eye and tell you that you ARE going to be okay, because I was where you are today and I made it through. There were days that I locked myself in my room, I cried on the floor, I cried alone and I cried in public. It may feel like you are going to die but you won't. As far as I know, no one has ever died from a broken heart so hang in there...This too shall pass.

Your relationship ended for a reason. The bigger reason may not be apparent to you just now but consider this: Perhaps he would have ended up cheating on you and you could have caught an incurable disease, perhaps the relationship would have taken a violent path or maybe staying in that relationship would have eventually broken your self esteem.

I think everyone should get a fair shot at love; I truly believe that everyone deserves that. They say that if you haven't had your heart broken then you haven't really opened up yourself fully to love. Living guarded is no way to live. Love is the greatest force in the world and once it's mutually shared then it's the most powerful and secure feeling in the world. Don't allow your Ex to rob you of that experience. Don't mess up your potential love life by holding on to the past. It may not feel like it now, but falling in love is worth the risk. It will take a lot of inner strength but you can do it. Love doesn't hurt...let me say that again...love does not hurt.

On the days that you really feel down remember that its all relative and no matter what you're going through it could be worse. You have to train yourself to look on the bright side! You now know the mistakes you've made in the past, you are now wiser and more capable of making better decisions regarding yourself, your future and any future mates. This is your chance to reinvent yourself! Use this time to discover who you are and learn something new about yourself. This will help you work on your issues in preparation for your next relationship. So many people are stuck in relationships that don't make them happy. You are free to start over; you have a new slate...appreciate that.

Chapter 8

Be Wiser

Be Wiser

The following is a few articles I wrote on my blog www.MissBaje.com that I want to share with you.

MR. GOOD ENOUGH

Often women settle with "Mr. Good", or "Mr. Good Enough"...robbing their selves of greatness. They ask themselves why cant I find Mr. Great, not realizing its because "Good" & "Good Enough" are in "Great's" bed!

You'll never get what you DESERVE until you let go of what you CURRENTLY have...Make room...and better will come. I promise you! You don't have to worry about whom and how...just make room!

Ps. It isn't going to be easy either, but it's necessary! There are going to be times when you second guess yourself   and times when you find yourself saying "but he's a good guy"...There are times you'll break a heart by walking away and yours may ache also in that walking away process...but you know WHAT?? What doesn't kill you makes you stronger. It doesn't mean you're lonely just because you're alone and it's better to be alone than in bad...or even "good enough" company.

The days you get worn down and feel like settling, think of all the sacrifices you made, the obstacles you've overcame, the struggles you endured and all your accomplishments as a woman; think of the man you want and the life you want. You deserve THE BEST...not mediocrity! You deserve someone who will PROFESS their love, PROTECT & PROVIDE, you deserve someone who will make you PROUD.

I made a promise long ago to never settle for less than I deserve...it hasn't been easy but today I can proudly say...I kept that promise :)

-MissBaje.com

<u>STARTING OVER NOW</u>

The great thing about life is ...you can start over any time you CHOOSE to. If you've been making the wrong decisions for the past 5 years, 10 years or all of your life, at any given moment you can CHOOSE to do things differently. You CAN go back to school, YOU CAN quit that job that stresses you out, and you CAN get out of that bad relationship TODAY!!!...LIFE COMES WITH A RESET BUTTON...IT'S CALLED "CHOICES"... Changing your life isn't easy, it takes *courage* and it takes *guts*...but you can do it! At first it will feel weird and a bit awkward. At times you may feel alone and sometimes it downright hurt like hell! But I promise you, I promise you... it will gradually get better...just find the courage within to take the first step :)

- MissBaje.com

APPRECIATE WHAT YOU DO HAVE

Some days when I feel a bit sad or under the weather I write a list of the things that I should be happy for...Like my health, my friends, my family, my home, and most of all my FREEDOM. Sometimes we get so stuck on minor things that go wrong in our lives and we don't realize that thousands of people actually have it much worse; NO food to eat, some people don't know where they'll sleep tonight, some people have absolutely NO family. Some people are in hospitals on life support fighting for their lives, some people can't walk on their own and need help to do *everything*. Some people are trapped in relationships that they are so unhappy in because of finances, or the fear of whatever... Today take a few seconds to celebrate the things that you SHOULD be happy about...and watch how that feeling of appreciation will make you value your day and life so much more.

-MissBaje.com

<u>YOU CAN DESIGN YOUR LIFE!</u>

Being in a relationship is a lot of responsibility and depending on what stage you are at in your life, it may be a bigger load than you can handle efficiently. When in a relationship you have to worry about how your decisions and actions will directly or indirectly affect your partner. You have to help them with their goals while you are working on yours. You often have to ask for permission for a lot of things or at the very least, *consider* how your mate would feel. You have to coordinate times schedules in order to spend time with each other… and the list goes on. It's a lot of work! The great news is now that you have all this available time and brain space you can use this time to create the life of your dreams! The world is yours! Whatever you can imagine you can make happen, *so make it happen!*

Perhaps you were in a relationship where your mate wasn't supportive of your goals, or perhaps you had to choose between going after your goals and being in a relationship. Perhaps you chose not to do a lot of things you wanted to do in order to make him happy. Maybe you wanted to go back to school, move to a different city, travel, change careers but you didn't because you were in a relationship...Well, now that you are single and have one less thing to worry about. It's time to tackle your goals!

Maybe you didn't have any goals outside of making that relationship work, and that's fine because the great thing about goals is you can create them and start working towards them at anytime. It may take some time to find out what your true passions are, (if your identity was lost in his, then it may take you a bit longer), but keep at it and keep experimenting until you find what you're good at and what truly makes you happy. This is your second chance at starting over!

If you need some help trying to choose what goal you should set or what dream you should go after then try this exercise. Think back, *way back*...to the days before you met him. What did you used to do before he came along? What use to light you up? In what hobbies did you partake? What did you used to dream about? What did you used to talk about doing *"some day"?* Make that *"some day"* "today"! You have the whole world waiting! Go get it girl!

Chapter 9

How to Pick Better Mates

How to Pick Better Mates

You can avoid the pain of a breakup simply by making the choice to make better choices about mates...

Maybe he was a good guy but he broke up with you; maybe you were a jealous lover. Maybe you were too controlling or possessive. Perhaps you were a bit insecure. As long as you realize it then you have the power to change it. I see it this way: people are who they are, if you have a problem with your mate hanging out with his friends because you think that he is going to cheat on you then that isn't a healthy relationship. Either you find a mate who you can trust or you need to work on your trust issues. You may ask: *'How do I know if it's my mate I can't trust or if I'm the one with the problem?'* You can find the answer to that by reflecting; Reflect on your past relationships and try to find the patterns.

For example, have most of the men you dated prefer to hang out with their boys most of the time than stay at home with you? If you had one or two like that then it may be a coincidence. *However* if ALL of your Exes displayed the same behavior then 1. You may just have a problem picking out compatible mates for yourself or 2. It may be something that you are doing or failing to do that is causing them to make those choices; It's all about cause and effect.

Don't get me wrong; if a man has cheated on you its never your fault. If a man has put his hands on you in a violent manner it is never your fault. But if *every single* man you've been with has cheated on you and has been violent with you, or if *every single* one of your Exes has had the same exact negative traits or all of your relationships ended for the *same exact* reason then you need to evaluate if your actions are contributing to the situation. Then ask yourself WHY do you keep choosing (in essence) the same kind of man.

I'm not saying that you are causing the men to act a certain way but you may be provoking what's already in them. When you first meet a man (way before you start dating him) you need to ask a few key questions. Here are some below:

Has he ever hit, shoved or choked a woman? If he has done it to other women don't expect to be the exception.

How is his relationship with his mother? The way he treats his mother is ultimately how he will treat you.

What are his personal and career goals? It's best to know the answers to these questions upfront to see if you are compatible long-term.

Does he watch a lot of sports? If he does then that will cut out a lot of the time you spend together. So if you're not into sports I suggest you find a hobby.

<u>FROM HERE FORWARD</u>

Set Your Own Goals - So that you don't end up at the "heartbreak hotel" again, enter your next relationship slowly. Don't make this person the sole focus of your entire life. Have your *own* goals and *own* life. Make a list of qualities and activities that you want to keep no matter who comes in your life.

Communicate - When you are starting a new relationship, it's important to communicate your intentions and requirements clearly with your partner. That way you can find out early on if they will be supportive and you will also avoid any misunderstandings.

Move Forward - Remember that everyman you'll meet is not your EX. Your rebound may be someone who really cares about you but if you're still bitter you may take it out on him; so don't judge your new guy by your Ex's mistakes.

THE BREAKUP GUIDE

Chapter 10

Your New Life Begins Now

Your New Life Begins Now

Guess what? You are writing this chapter! SURPRISE!! Yeah, you heard right! I gave you lessons, advice and tools for you to use over the next month and now that I've brought you as far as I can, its time for you to take over from here. You can do it!

Get a pen, (or a notebook if you're reading this as an E book) and start writing down your feelings. Write, write, and write! Write tips for yourself, write advice from others, write your favorite motivational quotes, write what you've done each day and more importantly write how you *feel*. I found writing to be therapeutic and hopefully you will too. Write your inner most feelings no matter how sad, disappointed, ashamed or angry you may be.

Let these pages be your safe haven for venting. Venting is like cleansing your soul. You can always destroy the pages after the thirty days are up, but keep it until then so you can track your progress over the next month.

Remember that reading this book alone will not help you. You have to actually partake in the activities that I suggest. After you have completed this last exercise feel free to write to me on day 30 and let me know if this book has helped you! iLoveBaje@Gmail.com

TAKE THE 30-DAY CHALLEGE!

Day 1

_____
_____
_____
_____
_____
_____
_____
_____
_____
_____
_____
_____
_____
_____
_____
_____
_____
_____
_____
_____
_____
_____
_____

"Never make guy a priority when you're only an option to him"

Day 2

_____
_____
_____
_____
_____
_____
_____
_____
_____
_____
_____
_____
_____
_____
_____
_____
_____
_____
_____
_____
_____
_____
_____

"The pursuit of love is always worth the risk"

Day 3

_____
_____
_____
_____
_____
_____
_____
_____
_____
_____
_____
_____
_____
_____
_____
_____
_____
_____
_____
_____
_____
_____
_____

"A new dawn brings a new day"

Day 4

_____
_____
_____
_____
_____
_____
_____
_____
_____
_____
_____
_____
_____
_____
_____
_____
_____
_____
_____
_____
_____

"It's never too late for a new beginning"

Day 5

_____
_____
_____
_____
_____
_____
_____
_____
_____
_____
_____
_____
_____
_____
_____
_____
_____
_____
_____
_____
_____

"You deserve someone who deserves you"

Day 6

_____
_____
_____
_____
_____
_____
_____
_____
_____
_____
_____
_____
_____
_____
_____
_____
_____
_____
_____
_____
_____

"There's plenty of fish in the sea. Throw that one back in and keep fishing!"

Day 7

_____
_____
_____
_____
_____
_____
_____
_____
_____
_____
_____
_____
_____
_____
_____
_____
_____
_____
_____
_____
_____
_____

"Your Ex was just a practice run"

Day 8

_____
_____
_____
_____
_____
_____
_____
_____
_____
_____
_____
_____
_____
_____
_____
_____
_____
_____
_____
_____
_____

"You don't have to settle"

Day 9

"You're worth it!"

Day 10

_____
_____
_____
_____
_____
_____
_____
_____
_____
_____
_____
_____
_____
_____
_____
_____
_____
_____
_____
_____
_____

"You have your whole life ahead of you"

Day 11

"Don't chase him, replace him"

Day 12

_____
_____
_____
_____
_____
_____
_____
_____
_____
_____
_____
_____
_____
_____
_____
_____
_____
_____
_____
_____
_____
_____
_____

"Men are like buses, every 15 minutes there's another one coming"

Day 13

_____
_____
_____
_____
_____
_____
_____
_____
_____
_____
_____
_____
_____
_____
_____
_____
_____
_____
_____
_____
_____
_____
_____

"They never really get it, until you're gone"

Day 14

_____
_____
_____
_____
_____
_____
_____
_____
_____
_____
_____
_____
_____
_____
_____
_____
_____
_____
_____
_____
_____
_____

"The best revenge is success"

Day 15

_____
_____
_____
_____
_____
_____
_____
_____
_____
_____
_____
_____
_____
_____
_____
_____
_____
_____
_____
_____
_____
_____

"You are more than enough"

Day 16

_____
_____
_____
_____
_____
_____
_____
_____
_____
_____
_____
_____
_____
_____
_____
_____
_____
_____
_____
_____
_____

"You'll never find another like him; you'll find better"

<u>Day 17</u>

_____
_____
_____
_____
_____
_____
_____
_____
_____
_____
_____
_____
_____
_____
_____
_____
_____
_____
_____
_____
_____
_____
_____

"It's his loss...seriously"

Day 18

_____
_____
_____
_____
_____
_____
_____
_____
_____
_____
_____
_____
_____
_____
_____
_____
_____
_____
_____
_____
_____

"Life's too short to waste on people who really don't matter"

Day 19

_____
_____
_____
_____
_____
_____
_____
_____
_____
_____
_____
_____
_____
_____
_____
_____
_____
_____
_____
_____
_____
_____
_____
_____
_____

"Your love is too precious to waste on some looser"

Day 20

_____
_____
_____
_____
_____
_____
_____
_____
_____
_____
_____
_____
_____
_____
_____
_____
_____
_____
_____
_____
_____
_____

"It has to rain for you to see a rainbow"

Day 21

"Nothing is holding you back...but you!"

Day 22

_____
_____
_____
_____
_____
_____
_____
_____
_____
_____
_____
_____
_____
_____
_____
_____
_____
_____
_____
_____
_____
_____

"No baggage, no drama...you are finally free"

Day 23

_____
_____
_____
_____
_____
_____
_____
_____
_____
_____
_____
_____
_____
_____
_____
_____
_____
_____
_____
_____
_____
_____
_____
_____

"Love does not hurt"

Day 24

_____
_____
_____
_____
_____
_____
_____
_____
_____
_____
_____
_____
_____
_____
_____
_____
_____
_____
_____
_____
_____
_____

"The world is at your fingertips"

Day 25

_____
_____
_____
_____
_____
_____
_____
_____
_____
_____
_____
_____
_____
_____
_____
_____
_____
_____
_____
_____
_____
_____

"Destiny doesn't happen by chance, it's by choice!"

Day 26

_____
_____
_____
_____
_____
_____
_____
_____
_____
_____
_____
_____
_____
_____
_____
_____
_____
_____
_____
_____
_____

*"There are two things you should never chase
behind: a bus and a man"*

Day 27

_____
_____
_____
_____
_____
_____
_____
_____
_____
_____
_____
_____
_____
_____
_____
_____
_____
_____
_____
_____
_____
_____
_____

"Once you know who you are, everything else falls into place"

Day 28

_____
_____
_____
_____
_____
_____
_____
_____
_____
_____
_____
_____
_____
_____
_____
_____
_____
_____
_____
_____
_____

"Just because you're alone doesn't mean you're lonely"

Day 29

_____
_____
_____
_____
_____
_____
_____
_____
_____
_____
_____
_____
_____
_____
_____
_____
_____
_____
_____
_____
_____

"Life is worth living"

Day 30

_____
_____
_____
_____
_____
_____
_____
_____
_____
_____
_____
_____
_____
_____
_____
_____
_____
_____
_____
_____
_____
_____
_____

"Don't be afraid your life will end, be afraid it will never begin"

CONCLUSION

I can't guarantee that you'll be completely over the breakup at day 30, but I will guarantee you that if you truly want to get over the breakup, if you take my advice to heart and if you whole heartedly try all the activities that I suggested, then you'll feel better than you did at day 1. I'm not telling you to do anything that I myself haven't tried. I'm not telling you to do anything that didn't work for me. In order for me to write a book like this to help you…I had to experience that awful emotion of sadness myself…and I did. I learnd my lessons and found what helped me and now I'm sharing it with you.

The mind frame and the activities that I am passing on to you have truly helped me. Getting back to your normal self will not always be easy…you will have to constantly train your mind to stay positive and productive…but it surely is possible. If you have to take the whole 30 day challenge over again to get your mind right then that's just what you have to do. Suck it up and jump right back in the game.

Come on! Let's do this!! Your new life is waiting!

: D   - Love Baje

If you need one-on-one advice send me an e-mail at ILoveBaje@gmail.com for my life coaching rates. I can coach you via e-mail, over the phone, through video chat or in person.

Subscribe to my blog MissBaje.com for updates, tips and giveaways.

To watch my free tutorials search me on Youtube.com /HeyThereBuddyBJ

Follow me on:

Twitter.com/ModelBaje

Facebook.com/MissBaje &

Instagram.com/MissBaje

IF YOU WANT TO HELP ME TO REACH MORE WOMEN YOU CAN DO SO BY LEAVING REVIEWS OF ALL MY BOOKS ON AMAZON!

IF YOU'RE APART OF A COMPANY, ORGANIZATION, GROUP, NON-PROFIT OR SORORITY AND WOULD LIKE TO BOOK ME FOR MOTIVATIONAL WORKSHOPS OR TO GIVE A MOTIVATIONAL SPEECHES DON'T HESITATE TO SEND ME AN E-MAIL.

IF YOU HAVEN'T READ MY FIRST BOOK YET 'A GOAL DIGGER'S GUIDE — HOW TO GET WHAT YOU WANT WITHOUT GIVING IT UP'...PLEASE READ IT AND IF YOU ALREADY HAVE READ IT YOU CAN ALWAYS BUY IT FOR ONE OF YOUR GIRLFRIENDS WHO CAN BENEFIT

FROM IT ;)

LOOKING FORWARD TO HEARING ABOUT YOUR PROGRESS!

-WITH LOVE,

MISS BAJE! YOUR LIFE DESIGNER